Creepy Bitches

Creepy Bitches:

Essays On Horror From Women In Horror

Edited by
Alyse Wax &
Rebekah McKendry, PhD

BearManor Media
2021

Creepy Bitches: Essays On Horror From Women In Horror

Edited by Alyse Wax and Rebekah McKendry, PhD

© 2021

All rights reserved.

No portion of this publication may be reproduced, stored, and/or copied electronically (except for academic use as a source), nor transmitted in any form or by any means without the prior written permission of the publisher and/or author.

Published in the United States of America by:

BearManor Media
1317 Edgewater Dr #110
Orlando FL 32804

bearmanormedia.com

Printed in the United States.

Typesetting and layout by John Teehan

Cover art by Karen McKenna

ISBN—978-1-62933-748-7

Contents

Foreword ix
    by Sandy Carpenter

A Monster With Many Faces

Meteorites and the Hillbillies Who Poke Them 3
    by Paula Haifley

The Mexican Monster Matriarchy: An Examination
of the Depiction of Female Monsters in Mexican
Horror Cinema of the 1950s and 1960s 11
    by Amy Voorhees Searles

What Found Me In the Woods 17
    by Kaydee Cage

Underground Horror: The New York City Subway
Scene and its Effect on my Daily Commute 23
    by Jenn Wexler

Horror Has Always Been a Smart Genre 29
    by Carly Lane-Perry

Taking the 'Ick' out of Ichthyology: Gender in the
Creature from the Black Lagoon Trilogy 35
    by Heather Hendershot

Adolescence and Horror

A Cure For Your Disco Problems 53
　　by Debbie Rochon

The Halloween Family 59
　　by Chelsea Stardust

The House That Dripped Dole Whip 65
　　by Erin Maxwell

The Ghosts of Berg's Video 73
　　by Rhianne Paz Bergado

The Bisexual Energy of *I Know What You Did Last Summer* Was a Peak 1990s Sexual Awakening 79
　　by Haleigh Foutch

Horror Lifestyle

David Cronenberg's Guide To Childbirth: Reflections On Being a Horror-Loving Parent 85
　　by Rebekah McKendry

Fashion and Fear: Where Diamonds, Denim and Decapitation Meet 95
　　by Zena Dixon

Food and Horror: An Unexpected Pairing 105
　　by Sarah Ann Stubbs

I'm Your Biggest Fan—Horror and Fandom

The X-Files, the Scully Effect, and the #metoo Movement 115
    by Alyse Wax

Elvira, Mistress of My Heart 129
    by Heidi Honeycutt

Passing Into Myth: *Candyman* and the Final Woman......137
    by Stacie Ponder

Trick 'R Treat..143
    by Shannon McGrew

Facing Your Fears

Learning To Love Home Invasion Horror Again After a Home Invasion......................................149
    by Meredith Borders

Cheap Scares: The Startle Effect and Community 155
    by Sonia Lupher

The Therapeutic Benefits of Horror for Those Suffering with Illness......................................163
    by BJ Colangelo

Monsters: Horror's Most Human Creatures 169
    by Jennica Lynn

Biographies..183

Foreword

by Sandy Carpenter

"...how was I terrified, when I viewed myself in a transparent pool! At first I started back, unable to believe that it was indeed I who was reflected in the mirror; and when I became fully convinced that I was in reality the monster that I am, I was filled with the bitterest sensations of despondence and mortification."[1]

RIVETED UNDER THE COVERS in the dark, my ten-year-old self could not tear myself away from the Frankenstein monster's sad tale. Abandoned by his creator, he wandered alone, eventually seeing himself as others saw him—a monster, an outsider to be feared, attacked and killed.

I was hooked.

In quick order, I picked up *Dracula*, followed by *The Island of Dr. Moreau*. Horror spoke to me. I was a loner who was born immune deficient and therefore spent a lot of time apart from others. I was a watcher. People seemed cruel to me and that grew into a fascination with the darkness that comes from within. Aliens and flying saucers never held much interest for me, but the things we're capable of doing to each other? Limitless.

And woman as terrifier? Now *that* was even more interesting. To this day, Mary Shelley is probably still my greatest influence. The duplicity of appearance versus interior thoughts seems...delicious.

Mary Wollstonecraft Shelley, Alice Guy Blanché, Daphne du Maurier, Alma Reville, Fay Wray, Hazel Court, Octavia Butler, Shirley Jackson, Janet Leigh, Ann Rice, Joyce Carol Oates, Verna Fields, Kay Rose, Kathryn Bigelow, Antonia Bird, Ve Neill, Mary Lambert, Jackie

---

1. *Frankenstein; Or The Modern Prometheus*. Mary Shelley. Vol 2, Chapter 4. First published by Lackington, Hughes, Harding, Mavor & Jones 1918.

Kong, Rachel Tallalay, Jamie Leigh Curtis, Debra Hill, Yoko Ogawa, Mira Grant, Alma Katsu, Xan Cassavetes, Mary Harron, Jen and Sylvia Soska, and Jennifer Kent. What do they have in common? They are all ages, races and nationalities. They are all women. And they are all Women in Horror.

Women and horror have been dancing partners since Mary Wollstonecraft Shelley birthed the monster *Frankenstein* two hundred years ago. Even earlier than Mary Shelley, Clara Reeve wrote *The Old English Baron* in 1777 and Ann Radcliffe wrote *The Mysteries of Udolpho* in 1794, now considered archetypal gothic horror.

The 1900s loosed more feminine horror. Marjorie Bowen wrote her first gothic horror novel about a medieval witch, *Black Magic*, in 1909. While she wrote historical novels under her own name, for her horror novels *Dr. Chaos* and *The Devil Snar'd*, she wrote under the pseudonym, George R. Preedy. Gertrude Barrows Bennett (writing as Francis Stevens) wrote *Citadel of Fear* and came to be considered one of the founders of the "weird tales" tradition. (And here all the comic nerds thought *Creepy* and *Eerie* were invented in the 1960s by Jim Warren and Jack Davis.)

The early 1900s brought a new medium to the story telling tradition: cinema. The first movies were shot by the companies who invented motion picture cameras and made the film that went in them to promote their products. In both France and the United States, these pioneers were women.

In France at Gaumont, a secretary named Alice Guy Blanché became the first woman to direct a film, and from 1896 to 1906 she was probably the only female filmmaker in the world. In 1903 she made "Faust et Mephistophales", a short film of only a few minutes duration. "The Pit and the Pendulum" followed in 1913, "The Monster and the Girl" in 1914, and "The Vampire" in 1915. Alice Guy Blanché is credited with being the first director to film a narrative story. Perhaps we can also consider her to be the founder of women in film horror.

In the United States, actress, director and producer Lois Weber made the 1913 thriller, "Suspense." This is notable in our history of women in horror because in 1914 she went on to make the first American feature film to be directed by a woman, *The Merchant of Venice*. She was also the first—and for many years, the only—woman elected to the Motion Picture Directors Association. It is through her narrative work in film that one can see the feminine eye for social issues and politics that carries on to this day in female creators' works.

Horror is a response, not a subject. A horror story is an allegorical medium for addressing larger social and personal issues. Through it we can explore our faith, our fears and the darkness that tears our souls. It is no coincidence that female creators in the genre are also often advocates or activists in social causes. I like to think my work in both film and comics fulfills the conscience of my ideals.

Fritz Lang's 1927 film, *Metropolis*, was a science fiction nightmare set in a futuristic utopian city which rests on the backs of abused workers. Germany of the 1920s was in the throes of severe economic depression and political chaos following World War I and the burden of a $33 billion debt in reparations it owed. Lang's film was the artist's way of commenting on the political realities and personal hardships of the German people. But it was a book, written in 1925, that the film was based on and that book and the subsequent screenplay were written by Lang's wife, Thea Von Harbou. High style by the filmmaker, but that style served a story of strife and suffering envisioned by a woman who also went on to produce the film.

Other women created works of horror in the subsequent decades. Interior, dark horror of the spirit with a commentary of the sociopathy of modern man.

The novelist Daphne du Maurier wrote dark tales from the 1930s to the 1960s including most famously the novella, *The Birds* in 1952. Alfred Hitchcock directed adaptations of her work including *The Birds* (1963), *Jamaica Inn* (1939), and *Rebecca* (1940).

Leigh Brackett, perhaps best known to film buffs for having written the Howard Hawks films *The Big Sleep* (1946) and *Rio Bravo* (1959), (or, if you're a millennial, *Star Wars: The Empire Strikes Back* [1980]), wrote the horror script, *The Vampire's Ghost*, for the 1945 Republic Films release. She started her career writing science fiction short stories and novels. Some of her stories have social themes, such as "The Citadel of Lost Ships" (1943), which considers the effects on the native cultures of alien worlds of Earth's expanding trade empire.

In 1953, Ida Lupino directed *The Hitchhiker*. The film is about two fishing buddies who pick up a mysterious hitchhiker during a trip to Mexico. Inspired by the crime spree of the psychopathic murderer Billy Cook (1928–1952), the screenplay was co-written by Lupino. Considered to be of the noir/crime genre, I believe that were it made today it would be considered a horror movie with a serial killer at its center.

Frankenstein (1931). *The Hunger* (1983). *Interview with the Vampire* (1994). *I Was a Teenage Frankenstein* (1957). *The Haunting* (1999). *Near*

Dark (1987). *Halloween* (1978). *Slumber Party Massacre* (1982). *Beloved* (1998). *The Accursed* (2010). *Pet Sematary* (1989). *Boxing Helena* (1993). *The Howling VI: The Freaks* (1991). *Freddy's Dead: The Final Nightmare* (1991). *Jaws* (1975). *Organ* (1996). *Ravenous* (1999). *Jennifer's Body* (2009). *American Psycho* (2000). *Twilight* (2008). *American Mary* (2012). *Soulmate* (2013). *My Soul to Keep* (2019). *Revenge* (2017). *Ginger Snaps* (2000). *The Babadook* (2014). These are iconic works of horror from the last two centuries. What they have in common besides that is the female creators involved in their realization either as writers, directors, producers, editors, sound effects editors or special effects make-up artists.

From the 1700s, women have been firmly rooted in the story telling tradition of horror. Why does "the fairer sex" venture into such messy territory? Perhaps it is because we who bring life into the real world are no strangers to the often violent, bloody roots of our very existence.

We are here. We are creators. We are undeniable in all our feminine glory as we tear your hearts out and spray your blood upon the walls.

A Monster With Many Faces

Meteorites and the Hillbillies Who Poke Them

by Paula Haifley

A SMALL BODY OF MATTER tumbles through the vast blackness of space towards a round blue planet, no particular agenda in mind. It feels no pain as it enters the atmosphere, heating and becoming incandescent light that streaks across the night sky. Landing softly, the now-small space rock nestles into the dirt under a canopy of trees, sweltering as it adjusts to its new environment. With no natural predators, the meteorite is quite surprised when it is suddenly and rudely poked with a stick by a good ole boy in a flannel shirt.

From backwoods country hayseeds to bloodthirsty cannibal rednecks, hillbillies have been a mainstay in cinema almost as long as they've been runnin' 'shine to the city folk. But how often do we think of the lovable bumpkin of science fiction, that bumbling boor who always pokes the meteorite he done found in the woods? Whether out of greed, curiosity, or pure dumb yokelness, this inciting character in overalls starts the hootenanny off right by releasing an alien who will conquer humanity.

The meteorite movie takes a left turn at the fork of the alien invasion film. When a cinematic UFO lands, out pops a hostile space force, psyched for human murder and domination, while a meteorite will just sit there cooling its cratered heels, waiting to be cracked open. These films also feature such stock sci-fi players as the Young Couple Making Out At Lovers' Lane Who Become Our Heroes; their Clueless Parents (or surrogate Useless Adults); and A Scientist Type Who Knows Stuff. So what makes the hillbilly the best firestarter, other than his ability to distill corn liquor that will put hair on your chest? These meteorite films aren't subtle in their political speechifying. Whether on the right or the left side of the pork barrel, they always feature an Alien Something trying to take over Anytown, USA, a metaphor for whatever has made the filmmakers as nervous as a long-tailed cat in a room full of rocking chairs. This threat has to start out small, a space rock no bigger than a minnow in a fishing hole which snowballs as it moves toward town where our hero(es) have to face and defeat the now terrifying off-world menace. So who's out there in the woods to begin with? Who's self-sustaining enough to hardly ever go to town, making him the ideal in-between? Whose inept bungling is predisposed to make us giggle? Why, it's your friendly local hillbilly! This rustic can be a hermit backwoodsman, a farmer who lives on the outskirts of the county, or a hunter who stumbles onto something he shouldn't have. The one thing these characters always have in common: they live separate lives from the average townsfolk, they always know how to find a stick, and they can't resist giving any space rocks a little nudge.

The pioneering "hillbilly poking a meteorite" film is 1958's *The Blob*. In this first incarnation, he's a denim and t-shirt clad coot living his best shack-in-the-woods life. When this old timer (Olin Howland) finds the smoking crater in the woods, he does what every modern horror audience would scream at him not to: he pokes it with a stick—repeatedly—probably for the entertainment, since his town doesn't even have a Walmart yet.

The meteorite opens, revealing the grey blob inside. This guy really goes hog wild on poking that blob until it climbs up the stick and onto his hand. Our hero, high school jock Steve (Steve McQueen) has been out in the woods parking with his date Jane (Aneta Corsaut) when they also see the meteor, and Steve decides to chase it. Since the old timer's hand is now completely encased in blob, he naturally pitches a fit and runs right in front of Steve's car, barely escaping being next on the menu at the roadkill cafe. Steve and Jane bring the old timer to the doctor who, since it's a small hamlet, operates out of his house. Thus, the hillbilly brings an interstellar monster from the backwoods into small town USA.

Steve is the polar opposite of the old timer, a clean-cut '50s teen who's the perfect young American. Steve's spotless persona typifies the ideal of the Eisenhower era, and the hillbilly, the one who exists between civilization and wilderness, has set Steve up to triumph over the evils of the foreign entity. Even the theme song "Beware of the Blob" reinforces how cool it is to be a square, upstanding citizen. You can practically smell the virginity and Brylcreem wafting off of the male chorus singers as they describe the Blob's behavior as if it's a new dance at the sock hop: "It creeps, and leaps, and glides, and slides across the floor. Right through the door." Pick a metaphor, folks, this movie will work for most: communism, juvenile delinquency, women wearing pants. But we're not here for political allegories; we're here for the hayseeds, so let's climb onto the wagon and keep moving.

American cinema's biggest contributor to the backwater yokel is none other than Stephen King himself, in 1982's *Creepshow*. Based on his short story "Weeds," King both wrote the segment "The Lonesome Death of Jordy Verrill" and also plays the lead in all of his bug-eyed, face slapping glory. In hindsight, we see that Verrill codified the meteorite-poking hillbilly for all subsequent films. Since he's the lead and spends most of the segment alone, we get to really dig into the what makes a backwoodsman tick, elevating this new stereotype from middling to high cotton. Verrill becomes the asteroid poking hillbilly *par excellence*. King devotes a page or so to the original *The Blob* in his 1981 non-fiction horror book *Danse Macabre*, saying, "The film has its genuine moments of unease and horror," and focusing largely on the demise of the old timer character. Even though "Jordy Verrill" riffs on the opening of *The Blob* with which King was clearly familiar, the character feels more like a love letter to the small-town Maine clodhopper who appears so often in King's fiction. And who better to portray the most corn-fed buffoon that has ever shown a red neck in science fiction than King himself?

Overall clad, unibrowed Verrill watches a shooting star fly over his farm shack, mugging like his life depended on a overacting contest. He runs into the woods, pulling a folding ruler out of his pocket and using it to prod the space rock. That's right, kids, Verrill is so on-brand that his stick collapses for easy travel. Verrill then gets so excited that he jabs the meteor with his fingers, burning them, and it is this bare-handed jostling that dooms him. Wanting to cool off the meteor so he can transport it to town, he accidentally cracks it in half, getting the blue goo inside it on himself and pouring it onto his land. Usually it takes a village to pull off a meteor invasion film, but in *Creepshow* the hillbilly acts as both the domino that starts the Rube Goldberg machine and the townsperson who brings the threat into civilization, making Verrill a one man alien virus spreading band. His action, instead of releasing a giant serving of Jello which will swallow movie theaters whole, creates the farmer's nightmare of an unstoppable invasive species.

Everything that the "meteor shit" has touched, including Verrill's skin, sprouts green weeds in the course of one night. When Verrill is completely covered with the space moss, he, and by extension his land, become the literal go-between, standing smack dab in the middle of the uncontrollable threat from space and the civilization of the nearest town. Not only did he release the genie from the bottle, but he will be its first victim. The fact that he doesn't even try to stop it proves that Momma Verrill did, in fact, raise idjits.

The meta, genre bending *The Adventures of Buckaroo Banzai Across the 8th Dimension!* (1984) turns the hillbilly and meteor's first date on its head. When the ally aliens come to earth in an organic-looking ship, it is almost immediately shot by two redneck hunters. Upon finding the disabled ship stuck in a tree, one pokes at the branches with a stick. The ship opens and the first alien spills out and dies, leading the bewildered hunters to call the authorities. This gets Buckaroo to the scene, thus serving the meteor poking hillbilly's purpose of delivering otherworldly contents to our protagonist.

In 1986's *Night of the Creeps*, another self-aware genre tribute, the hillbilly/meteor status quo is even more subverted, with frat boys being the outsider to our protagonists' nerds and townies dream team. In the 1959-set prologue, sorority co-ed Pam (Alice Cadogan) is out parking with frat boy Johnny (Ken Heron). When the couple sees that fatal shooting star, like Steve McQueen before him, Johnny decides to chase it. The couple drives to an isolated road, and Johnny leaves Pam in the car while he traipses through the woods, uncovering the freshly landed intergalactic debris. Just as he's about to touch it, the glass canister breaks and a space worm flies into Johnny's mouth, possessing him with an escaped alien science experiment.

Instead of the hillbilly bringing the threat from the wilderness to civilization, it's the handsome McQueen-type that brings the threat from the square 1950s to the post-modern 1980s, by way of a cryogenics chamber. In *Creeps*, it's the mindless Greek college culture that starts the infection, and the nerds trying to fit into that culture that release it into the city, by getting Johnny's body out of the science lab freezer as a hazing prank for a fraternity that never intended to have them as members. Our heroes have to stop the literal mindless zombies (dead bodies reanimated by space worms), created out of metaphorical mindless zombies (drunken frat boys), from their mission to slaughter co-eds that naturally ensues.

By the time the 1988 remake of *The Blob* rolls around, literal hillbillies are far out of fashion, leaving the homeless to fill their flannel. This film's hobo (Billy Beck) is living in the woods in a hovel, staking his claim to the transitional lands between the wilderness and civilization. The hobo goes to investigate the meteorite, and as in the original, he pokes the blob with a stick. This modern blob scoots up the stick and onto the hobo's hand quickly and aggressively, making him panic. When he encounters a teen from town in the woods, it's juvenile delinquent Brian (Kevin Dillon) who tries to help. The hobo runs into the road, and this time football hero Paul (Donovan Leitch) hits him with the car. Paul, his cheerleader date Meg (Shawnee Smith), and Brian take the wounded man to the hospital, so both the teen dream and the bad boy carry the monster across the threshold to the populated area. The evolution of '50s backwoodsman to '80s hobo puts the character on the very outskirts of a country feeling the effects of Reaganomics, filling the disposable man role with someone who'd be all but ignored by most of society.

The hobo brings the threat from his self-made shack straight into a tourist ski town that's in the grips of a recession (due to lack of snow). Once the Blob starts to spread, it's the outsiders that take the lead, leaving the golden boy jock of the '50s behind, both literally and metaphorically a relic. It is the hillbilly type that continues to evolve film to film, and thus persists. In the late '80s our leads become juvenile delinquents and cheerleader action heroes, but our meteor poking outsiders will always be there on the fringes.

In *Killer Klowns From Outer Space* (1988), it's not a meteor that the farmer finds after seeing what he thinks is Halley's Comet landing in the woods, but a circus tent. Farmer Gene Green (Royal Dano) punches the circus tent after the Klowns take his dog, upping the ante from a standard poke to a good what-for. The big top repels him, so he yanks on the tent ropes, electrocuting himself and becoming the Klowns' first human victim. Meanwhile, the young couple who were out necking in the woods also decide to find the comet. Once they spy the Klown tent, their curiosity leads them to explore the inside, where they find Gene's dead body encased in cotton candy. The couple narrowly escapes being the next to die and run to town. The Klowns naturally follow, terrorizing and cotton candy-ing the citizens. Thus it is the hillbilly's death that moves the slaughter along, again creating a new twist on the standard for these modern times of the 1980s.

Speaking of genre subversion, 2006's *Slither* turns the hillbilly trope completely around. The meteorite lands in the woods outside the small town of Wheesly, populated almost entirely by rednecks and farmers, established by quick shots of hunting stores, confederate flags, and a banner for the deer season kick-off party. The meteorite opens on its own once it hits the dirt, but it is the town's lone rich man, Grant Grant (Michael Rooker) who pokes the grey blob that has oozed out, making the alien parasite skedaddle directly into Grant's body. Echoing the themes of *Night of the Creeps*, in Wheesly it is the highfalutin' who are the instigators. Grant's hunger for sex leads him into the woods with a woman who isn't his wife (who herself hungers for his money), and then the greed of the aliens turn the locals into either infected hosts of the space parasite, spawners knocked up with alien seed, or food for both. It is the redneck Sheriff Pardy (Nathan Fillion) and the formerly poor school teacher Starla Grant (Elizabeth Banks) who join forces to save what's left of their cattywampus town.

Tangentially related are three films based on H. P. Lovecraft's short story "The Colour Out Of Space," about a meteor that lands on a backwoods farm and starts to taint the water, the land, and then the crops. 1987's *The Curse* and 2010's *Die Farbe* feature meteorites being found by farmers, but in both cases the hillbillies show more sense than Verrill and call in a scientist or doctor to investigate. In 1965's *Die Monster Die!*, the meteorite has been secreted away in an old manor house years before the film even begins, so the irradiated space junk has been mutating things to its heart's content before the hero even knows it exists. Each film uses the meteorite as a metaphor for decay and corruption of the family unit, whether by the cruelty of the husband/step-father (*The Curse*), the turmoil leading up to World War II in Germany (*Die Farbe*), or the crumbling English gentry (*Die Monster Die!*). *Deadly Spawn* (1983) also forgoes the hillbilly, with the shooting star releasing its giant three-headed dick monster on its own, which almost immediately finds its way to suburban New Jersey to eat people. These films don't move any space varmints closer to town, but keep them on the outskirts, just as they're on the outskirts of this chapter.

In 1997's *Men In Black*, Edgar (Vincent D'Onofrio) is a serious Jordy Verrill, and the ultimate ornery redneck stereotype: a pickup truck driving, overalls wearing rural farmer who browbeats his wife. When a fiery UFO crashes on his property, he goes out to greet it with a shotgun. Thus the hillbilly comes full circle, from old harmless coot who pokes things with a stick to the young, dumb and full of bile hayseed who approaches a crater ready to blast any meteor shit into oblivion. When the unseen alien asks Edgar to set his weapon down, he replies "You can have my gun when you pry it from my cold, dead fingers," and the evolution of how America sees its country cousins is complete. The alien kills Edgar and puts on his skin, showing yet again an alien menace using a rube to jump from the outskirts of society to a populated area, only this time the alien is smart enough to skip the suburbs and head straight for the big city.

Finally, we get to 2018's *Rampage*. Yes, this film actually fits the theme, it's not just included to make jokes about an ape being smarter than a pastoral stereotype. George is also someone who lives on the outskirts. A rare albino gorilla whose entire family was slaughtered by poachers, he's become best friends with someone of a different species, the primatologist (Dwayne Johnson) who rescued him and is now his zookeeper. George lives in a forested enclosure in a wildlife sanctuary, cohabiting with other gorillas, but is remarkable in the differentness of his looks, his intelligence, and his relationship to his human. George watches something fall from the sky onto his land and goes to investigate it. As curious as his namesake from children's literature, he gives the canister he finds the ceremonial poke. It sprays him in the face with a genetically modified pathogen that causes him to both grow to enormous size and become aggressive, thus making him the alien menace who threatens humanity. Like Verrill before him, he is the inciting incident that then morphs into the threat itself. Unlike Verrill, he is given a chance to find redemption and then save the very humanity he had been threatening. Plus, who doesn't like to see a simian joking around with The Rock?

Over and over again, these meteorite films, like *Invasion of the Body Snatchers* before them, use Small Town America as the stage to fight an outside threat that could overtake the country, even the world. And the hillbilly is always there to prop open humanity's door, using a stick he found in the woods as a doorstop. This corn-fed yokel is still treated as a relative innocent, a sylvan child of nature, because he exists in the in-between: he has to bring the infestation from the outside through to the inside. Even though he's the one letting those little ole space doggies in, we can't fault science-fiction's hillbilly for just doing his job. Without this corn-fed figure wandering the outskirts of the civilized town, we'd be stuck with a movie about whiny teenagers who saw a shooting star once.

The Mexican Monster Matriarchy: An Examination of the Depiction of Female Monsters in Mexican Horror Cinema of the 1950s and 1960s

by Amy Voorhees Searles

THERE IS A COMMON MISCONCEPTION that, when audiences demand "strong female characters," they are looking for black belt astrophysicists with perfect hair. This is patently ridiculous. Any type of female character has the potential to be "strong" as long as they are rendered in three dimensions. It is no secret that many fans of horror cinema consider themselves outcasts and, as such, are often able to identify with the monsters or antagonists in these films. Whether one relates to the tragically misunderstood Frankenstein's monster, or the primal anger of Jason Voorhees, these fantastical depictions of a viewer's inner turmoil can provide a valuable—and entertaining—catharsis. Therefore, just as all marginalized demographics yearn for representation in popular culture, so too must fully realized female monsters be included. During the 1950s and 1960s, while filmmakers in the United States did their part to contribute various she-creatures, a wrathful severed head, and all manner of bad seeds, Mexico's comparatively small film industry rivaled the U.S. in the production of monstrous femininity.

With a few notable exceptions, such as *El Fantasma del Convent* (*The Phantom of the Convent*, 1934), *Dos Monjes* (*Two Monks*, 1934), and *El Misterio del Rostro Pálido* (*The Mystery of the Ghastly Face*, 1935), horror did not truly find its place in the Mexican cinematic landscape until the late 1950s. Up until that point, melodramas, westerns, and comedies dominated the screen. However, after the surprising box office success of *El Vampiro* (*The Vampire*, 1957), the floodgates were open. At that time, William Jenkins, an American entrepreneur who made his fortune in Mexico, owned approximately 80 percent of the movie theaters in the country. This monopoly allowed Jenkins and his business associates to mandate that content should have mass market appeal in order to better serve their financial interests, even though this decree regularly clashed with the state's demand for didactic material that reinforced the government's ideological messaging. The Mexican film industry's response to the public's (and Jenkins') growing appetite for horror films spawned numerous violent ape-men, ambulatory voodoo dolls, and, famously, a brain-eating baron. But strikingly, it also produced a preponderance of wicked women, the reasons for which—as with any cultural phenomenon—are multivalent.

One of the prevailing political tenets in the wake of the Mexican Revolution was the promotion of *indigenismo*: a movement meant to empower and celebrate the people indigenous to the territory prior to Spain's colonization of Mexico. One of the native tribes, the Aztecs, was polytheistic, and a brief survey of their pantheon reveals why women may more naturally be associated with horrific themes in Mexico. The earth goddess Coatlícue, with a face composed of twin serpents and adornments made of writhing snakes and human remains, symbolizes both life and death; for just as the earth mother gives life to us all, so too must she devour all that lives. Mictlanciuatle, the skull-faced queen of the land of the dead, guards the bones of the deceased and oversees festivals for the dead. These Aztec festivals evolved into the modern day *Día de Muertos*, and echoes of Mictlanciuatle can still be seen today in the bony visage of the popular folk saint Santa Muerte. The deity Cihuacóatl, a snake woman dressed in white who embodies fertility, was said to have abandoned her son at a crossroads. Remorsefully, she would routinely return to this spot to cry for her lost child. This myth functions as a clear antecedent to *La Llorona*.

Perhaps Mexico's chief horror export is the lore of *La Llorona* (otherwise known as The Crying Woman). Evidence of her penetration into the present-day consciousness of the U.S. can be seen from such disparate sources as multiple mazes at Universal Studios Hollywood's Halloween Horror Nights, to her appearance as an adversary in the *Batwoman* comic books. While innumerable iterations of the folktale exist, the predominant narrative is similar to that of Medea. Typically, the story concerns a young mother who has been abandoned or otherwise betrayed by the father of her children. To exact revenge on him—and often to spare her offspring from poverty or humiliation—she drowns her children. This heinous act, coupled with her profound remorse, doom her to forever wander the earth, wailing, in search of her lost progeny. In true bogeywoman fashion, this woman in white menaces careless children who, in crossing her path, may be claimed as substitutes for the little ones she lost. Considering the folktale's prevalence, it was natural that La Llorona would be the subject of one of Mexico's first horror films: *La Llorona* (*The Crying Woman*, 1933). It also follows that this fount of fear would be revisited during the horror boom of the '50s and '60s, and the period birthed both *La Llorona* (*The Crying Woman*, 1960) and *La Maldición de la Llorona* (*The Curse of the Crying Woman*, 1961).

Another supernatural hallmark of Latin American culture, with both deep pre-Columbian roots and a rich folkloric history is *Brujería* (witchcraft). Though *Brujería* can be practiced by members of any gender, it is primarily linked with *brujas* (female witches). After the Spanish colonized Mexico, practitioners of *Brujería* were persecuted, as their system of belief was deemed incompatible with Christianity. In spite of this oppression, *Brujería* persisted, evolved, and even incorporated elements of Catholicism into its rituals. Although the government's post-Revolution stance was that indigenous culture should be venerated and promoted, a negative stigma remained bound to the spiritual and healing traditions of *Brujería*. Therefore, *brujas* (and occasionally, *brujos*) were repeatedly employed as the frightful foes or cruel catalysts of Mexican horror screenplays. Examples of this can be seen in films such as *Misterios de la Magia Negra* (*Mysteries of Black Magic*, 1958), *El Espejo de la Bruja* (*The Witch's Mirror*, 1962), *Los Jinetes de la Bruja* (translated literally as *The Witch's Riders*, 1966), *Las Mujeres Panteras* (*The Panther Women*, 1967), and *Atacan las Brujas* (*Santo in The Witches Attack*, 1968).

With *Brujería* chiefly identified with women, Aztec beliefs that represent maternity and mortality as the dual nature of many of their goddesses, and female symbols serving as the physical embodiment of death (Santa Muerte, or her secular counterpart, La Catrina), it seems reasonable that women would be perceived as more predisposed to the supernatural, or more sensitive to communication from beyond the veil. This concept is explored in a number of ways across a variety of films. In *Espiritismo* (*Spiritism*, 1962), only women are shown to have access to mediumistic powers. In *La Momia Azteca* (*The Aztec Mummy*, 1957), a woman is the only one willing to undergo hypnosis and regress to a former life. Similarly, in *Santo en el Tesoro de Drácula* (*Santo and Dracula's Treasure*, 1969), only women are physically capable of traveling into their past lives. In *El Libro de Piedra* (*The Book of Stone*, 1969), a young girl is the only one able to commune with a long dead occult emissary.

The mental resolve and physical strength demonstrated by the heroines in some of the titles above may have its origins in the Mexican Revolution. During the conflict, in addition to more traditional tasks like nursing and cooking, many women served as *soldaderas*, soldiers who not only participated in combat, but also commanded troops and oversaw important military incursions. The Constitution of Mexico (*Constitución Política de los Estados Unidos Mexicanos*), drafted in response to the Mexican Revolution, guaranteed equal rights for women under Article 4. The PRI (*Partido Revolucionario Institucional*), the political party that governed Mexico after the war, recognized that cinema was a valuable means of cultural transmission, and so they established state sponsorship and regulation for the film industry. Under the aegis of the PRI, Mexican cinema propagated doctrines central to the Revolution (such as *indigenismo*, mentioned previously) as well as codes of behavior, all couched within an accessible and entertaining pastime. When it came to a woman's place in society however, there were conflicting objectives. On one hand, due to the gender equality espoused in the new Constitution, modern women were to be presented as capable and morally upstanding. On the other, the country's new leadership had a vested interest in maintaining the patriarchal system. This ideological schism conceivably explains the number of films featuring malevolent female space invaders. Movies like *La Nave de los Monstruos* (*The Ship of Monsters*, 1960), *El Planeta de las Mujeres Invasoras* (*Planet of the Female Invaders*, 1966), *Arañas Infernales* (*Hellish Spiders*, 1968), and *Blue Demon y Las Invasoras* (*Blue Demon vs. The Diabolical Women*, 1969) accomplish the feat of presenting powerful female characters, while simultaneously promulgating pro-patriarchal and anti-colonialist sentiment.

As evidenced by these *invasoras*, one crucial distinction between the female movie monsters generated by Mexico as compared to those created in the United States is that their monstrosity is either inherent to the character or purposely sought after through voluntary pacts with the powers of darkness. In the U.S. productions, the female monster is more often victimized; the result of the intervention of male mad scientists or sinister hypnotists. This can be witnessed in *The She-Creature* (1956), *Frankenstein's Daughter* (1958), and *The Brain That Wouldn't Die* (1962), to name but a few.

Of course, if the primary function of women in Mexican horror cinema was to portray repulsive beasts or disciples of evil, the rank misogyny on display would make for uncomfortable viewing. But just as the female monsters appear to have more agency than their neighbors to the north, so too do the female protagonists in these films. From the ambitious and self-possessed journalist of *El Monstruo Resucitado* (*Monster* or *The Revived Monster*, 1953) to the myriad crime fighting *luchadoras* (female wrestlers) in movies like *Las Luchadoras Contra el Médico Asesino* (*Doctor of Doom*, 1963), women seem just as likely to play the hero as the villain. Even more important than these two poles, though, is the fact that women occupy diverse positions in these horror narratives. Within a single film, various women could serve as tragic victim, noble hero, and supernatural menace. This is the case in *El Espejo de la Bruja* (*The Witch's Mirror*, 1962), and is particularly conspicuous in *Hasta el Viento Tiene Miedo* (*Even the Wind is Afraid*, 1968), as almost every character in the film is female.

Due to this wealth of "strong female characters"—especially those that are monstrous or murderous, or that play a role more generally aligned with masculinity—the Mexican horror and exploitation films of this era testify that they are worthy of rediscovery and reevaluation through a modern lens.

Though linked for their thematic content and entertainment value more so than their potential for cultural enlightenment, the following double features—each containing one entry from Mexico and one from the United States, from the time period germane to this essay—have been compiled to help guide the reader through the wonderful world of weird women.

- *La Bruja* (*The Witch*, 1954) / *The Wasp Woman* (1959)
- *La Momia Azteca* (*The Aztec Mummy*, 1957) / *The She-Creature* (1956)
- *La Mujer y la Bestia* (*The Woman and the Beast*, 1959) / *Strait-Jacket* (1964)
- *La Nave de los Monstruos* (*The Ship of Monsters*, 1960) / *Queen of Blood* (1966)
- *La Maldición de la Llorona* (*The Curse of the Crying Woman*, 1961) / *Daughter of Dr. Jekyll* (1957)
- *El Espejo de la Bruja* (*The Witch's Mirror*, 1962) / *She Demons* (1958)
- *Santo vs. las Mujeres Vampiro* (*Samson vs. the Vampire Women*, 1962) / *Blood of Dracula* (1957)
- *La Cabeza Viviente* (*The Living Head*, 1963) / *The Brain That Wouldn't Die* (1962)
- *Arañas Infernales* (*Hellish Spiders*, 1968) / *Spider Baby* (1967)
- *La Señora Muerte* (*Madam Death*, 1969) / *The Leech Woman* (1960)

What Found Me In the Woods

by Kaydee Cage

This transcript was taken from a recording found inside a camera in an abandoned farmhouse in rural Maryland near Kennedyville. The video identified the speaker as Kaydee Cage, a local farmer who went missing four years ago from her home in Barlowe, about twenty miles away. The video feed cut out as she opened the door to let another person in, and although audio continued uninterrupted, it is unknown to whom Cage was speaking. The authenticity of the recording has been neither verified nor debunked by forensic investigators.

As of this writing, the whereabouts of Kaydee Cage and the identity of the other occupant in the room remain unknown. If you have any information about her disappearance, please contact the Kent County Sherriff's Office at (667) 555-3253

OH HEY, IT'S YOU. Where have you been? Come in, quickly. Let me bolt that door behind you. There. Can't be too careful. Not now, anyway. Better settle in right over there. That's it. Warm yourself by the fire. A farmhouse this old doesn't have any heat as far as I can tell, so I've stayed right here. It looks like we're going to be here a while longer. What's happening out there now? I've been holed up here for hours now. Oh, you can't speak? Okay, don't panic. At first, I couldn't either. Your voice will come back in time.

Oh my God, when she looked at me. It just froze me on the spot. Luckily Pepper bit her before it was too late. My dog bit a real-life witch! Who would believe that? Well, I'm calling her a witch, anyway. I'm not exactly sure what she was but 'witch' is as good a word as any to describe that thing.

I was out there in the woods walking Pepper and out of nowhere she was just…there. The stench of her hit me first. What WAS that smell? It turned my stomach. And the bodies of those poor people. What was she doing with them?

Before I knew it I was looking into those black eyes, and I couldn't move. That's when Pepper attacked her. She broke eye contact, and I ran. I heard Pepper howling in pain, but I couldn't go back for him. I couldn't even bring myself to look back. I owe that dog my life.

I just kept running in a full panic. I remember coming across more bodies and that's when you saw me. I ran right past you, but my voice was still gone so I couldn't warn you about what I was running from. Anyway, I came out of the woods at nightfall and I've been here ever since. This whole thing must have started a few days ago. Those other bodies had been there awhile.

What's that? You mean the camera? Yes, it's on. It's recording everything in this room. Look, if we don't make it out of here, people are going to want to know what's happening. That camera may be the only record of this event, so we need to tape everything. If something does happen to us, I only hope someone finds the footage of the strange things that have occurred in the last few days. You know, like a found footage horror movie.

Oh yeah, I love found footage. Well I *did* anyway. It's a completely different experience when it's happening to you. But I've seen more than a few. That's why I thought to start taping so early on. Yeah, I know. We've all seen a found footage movie by now, but you know what this situation reminds me of? Well, being stuck in a very real ordeal like we are, living in fear of the unknown, I'm recalling the one and only time I watched found footage and believed it was the real thing. I mean, this thing really scared me. *Me*. A grown woman. I'll tell you about it. We've got time to kill, and I've been sitting here talking to myself for too long.

It was midsummer of 1999. I was minding my own business, flipping channels, when I caught a documentary called *Curse of the Blair Witch*. By now everyone's heard of the Blair Witch. Back then, though? It was the Orson Welles' *War of the Worlds* radio broadcast for a new generation. To be honest, I bought it pretty easily. I am not an unintelligent woman, but I was pretty naïve, essentially being 'punked' by a fictitious documentary. Um, spoilers ahead. But who cares? If we make it out of this, my guess is neither one of us will watch another horror movie again.

So, this documentary began with a short narration explaining who the woman that would come to be known as the Blair Witch was, what she was accused of doing to be branded a witch, and what happened to the townsfolk after they banished her and left her to die in the nearby woods. I can't remember her name offhand, but I think it was an E name. Elsa, Edith, Elly. That's it. Elly-something. What a creepy intro. Then they showed some footage from this thing called *The Blair Witch Project*. At the time, I'm asking myself, what *is* this? Who are these people? Did something happen to them?

Apparently, they went off into the woods near Burkittsville, Maryland to search for this witch from some local folklore. Then they proceeded to disappear from the face of the earth. There were interviews with law enforcement, as well as family and friends of the missing students. They showed news stories about the search parties coming up empty. Honestly, it was all so thoroughly edited together, I was hooked. It was very unsettling. Look, I'm getting goosebumps just thinking about it. Are you still with me? Good, because it just gets creepier.

Next, they told this entire backstory of all the mysterious goings-on. Murders, disappearances, strange happenings—all around Burkittsville. But it was the way these stories were presented that made me believe them. My favorite? That would be the grainy 1971 documentary by Andromeda Productions called *Mystic Occurrences*, featuring a modern-day witch explaining parts of the Blair Witch legend. It didn't ever occur to me it was a fabrication. It just looked and sounded like a cheesy 1971 documentary. There were a couple other things they did that convinced me it was all for real. There was this book discovered called the uh...*The Blair Witch Cult*, I think. Presumably it contained many accounts of people encountering the witch. That's not what interested me. It was the folklore professor claiming it was all lies, along with the Burkittsville historian claiming it was mostly factual, that impressed me. By making each one look like a liar about the contents of the book, I didn't even consider there was no book in the first place. How is that for manipulation?

There was one other scene involving the folklore professor that worked really well. He poked holes in the logic of one of the stories that supposedly happened. Not every story. Just this one in particular. So instead of claiming it's all fake, he threw just a little bit of doubt at the audience. I mean, think about it: if someone is trying to get you to believe a big lie, wouldn't it work better if you told lots of little ones? Then you can say, 'well sure, only this part here is outrageous, so the rest could still be true, right?' Not only did it work perfectly on me, it freaked me right out.

And here's the kicker: they explained how and where their film footage was found. They showed how the backpacks with all the camera stuff was found several years later in an impossible location: buried under a colonial era wall. I mean, these guys really did their homework. I'm telling you, the marketing campaign for *The Blair Witch Project* was so well done, so detailed, it sucked me right in and wouldn't let go. So of course, I *had* to see the movie when it came out. After watching the documentary, I went to bed that night and imagined the Blair Witch was right there, outside my bedroom window. Waiting for me. I can still hear her…

Well, that's the story of my first introduction to found footage horror. But you know, there's more to the love affair between me and found footage than just a documentary about a witch. Do you have time for one more story? Ha ha, I know. We're not going anywhere. Do you feel like you can speak yet? No? All right, where was I? Ah yes. The actual movie.

I found out it was fake right before I saw it in the theater. Curiosity killed the cat, hon. I grabbed a local newspaper and read the review. That was it. The review spoiled it all. If I was going to spill the beans about a movie, I'd give a spoiler alert. They gave away everything. They were actors using their real names. There was no witch. It was just a movie. Of course it was fake, right? Witches, please. After reading that article my common sense gradually began to filter through the fog of uncertainty. *Curse of the Blair Witch* was a straight-up brainwash. If it had been a cult, I would have been hippie-dancing in the forest, plotting her return.

But here's the strange part. I absolutely loved the movie. No, really. I mean, I know it wasn't real, but it was still creepy as hell. It was shot realistically, but it wasn't trying to fool me anymore. I'd moved past that conceit with my Little-Miss-Nosy approach to film appreciation. Somehow, on its own merit, it was exactly the kind of movie I wanted to see. After the lights came on, I turned around and saw these two slightly older women, much like us now, still sitting there in shock with their hands covering their mouths. At that moment I thought to myself, *it worked*.

Look at the characters. It was their fallibility that made it real for me. Take us for example. Here we are, two women forced to be strong in a bad situation. The leader in the film, Heather, had the same duty. She was headstrong and at the outset of their trip, completely unaware of her own flaws. She had to deal with the unknown, which brought out her strengths and her weaknesses. I got the impression we were witnessing real people, fighting against a supernatural being, or at least the idea of a supernatural being. I loved that. And it was still scary.

Oh look, it's daybreak. Thank God. Once the sun is up—completely up, we're not taking any chances—we're getting out of here in the pontoon. Are you OK? You don't look so good. Do you want to lie down for a while? It's a long boat ride across the bay to Havre de Grace. You're good? Well I'm not sleeping either. Not with that… whatever it is in the dark out there. So, since we're still here I'll finish up my story.

I must have seen at least one hundred found footage movies by now and I know what it is I love so much about them. Remember, it's not whether I thought it was real or not. I've never believed any of them were real after *Curse*. What I like about found footage is the danger feels more real when filtered through the subject's own lens. And an uncut camera panning around is one of the best ways to get a jump scare. The handheld style works well with the likes of ghost hunting movies like *Grave Encounters*, where the characters would be expected to walk around with cameras, filming everything. Setting up static cameras is a great found footage trick as well. If you can give a good reason to be filming in the first place, you're halfway there.

The mockumentary is one of my favorite subsets of found footage. *Curse of the Blair Witch* ensured that. Ever seen *Lake Mungo*? It's one of the best horror documentaries out there. Extremely haunting. Stuck with me for days.

But my absolute favorite thing about found footage is this: there is almost no chance for a happy ending. I think a good horror story should generally avoid ending on a positive note. Most of the time, something bad had to have happened to the person operating the camera. Someone else needs to find it later for the whole premise to work.

Found footage is a hidden art form. Most of my favorites were discovered by hard target searches and strong word of mouth. There are some amazing gems out there. After seeing so many of them, I've come to look at found footage not as a genre, but a style of filmmaking. All the traditional horror genres have been given the found footage treatment. Monsters? *Digging Up the Marrow*. Giant monsters? *Cloverfield*. Vampires? *Afflicted*. Serial Killers? *Creep*. Horror comedy *and* vampires? *What We Do in the Shadows*. Bigfoot? *Exists*. Anthology? *V/H/S*. Even sci-fi/horror is represented with *Devil's Pass*. Up until a few days ago, I loved the 'scary woods at night' movies and there's plenty of them as well.

My favorite is the paranormal stuff. Ghosts, hauntings, abandoned asylums or hotels. *Hell House LLC* was the best in that bunch. You know, when I think back—do smell that? Hey, are you all right? Why are you looking at me like that? Jesus. It's *you*. Stay away DEAR GOD PLEASE NO I DON'T WANT TO DIE! I DON'T WAN—(*indecipherable sound*)

Underground Horror: The New York City Subway Scene and its Effect on my Daily Commute

by Jenn Wexler

BEING PUSHED ONTO THE TRACKS. Getting assaulted on a lonely car in the middle of the night. *Manspreading*. The subway is a terrifying place. As a New Yorker, it's also my prime source of transportation. And so, I've come to know and fear the subway intimately.

I'm also a filmmaker and a horror fan, so this is perhaps a way to cope with my metro-related anxieties. I mean, it is an intertwining maze of tunnels atop a Lovecraftian abyss, right? And for the past few years I've been seeking out and cataloging horror movie scenes set on and in the New York City transit system.

While I hold many scary movie subgenres dear to my heart, the Horror Movie Subway Scene speaks to me deeply, offering a strange kind of pride and a certain amount of ownership; like this fear belongs to *me*. I've *earned* it. I face it every time I come home late and have to walk an empty subway platform. I've looked that horror right in the face that time I unexpectedly stepped onto a train car to see a creep-dude masturbating.

When waiting for what feels like forever on the platform, or on never-ending rides uptown, I think about these horror movie scenes. I meditate on them. I sometimes place myself inside of them, and daydream (day-nightmare?) about what I would do if one of these situations broke out in my subway car at that very moment. (Hey, we all have our ways to pass the time.)

These are the stops on that mental underground, the horror movie moments that have freaked me out the most, and which have shaped my love/hate relationship with the best/worst subway system in the world. Come ride along with me…

MANIAC (1980)

William Lustig's *Maniac* is the movie that made me realize my fascination with subway scenes. Joe Spinell stars as a serial killer with mommy and mannequin issues who stalks the streets of New York on the hunt for his victims. One night, he follows a young nurse down below 59th Street and Columbus Circle. Sensing that the shady figure down the platform is after her, the nurse hurries into the subway bathroom to hide, which of course is where she meets her death. This scene is the reason (ok, *one* reason) why I never go into the bathroom at subway stations. It also helps me justify taking cabs home after 10pm.

Lustig uses the already-scary attributes of the station to heighten the tension: Dutch angles in the stairwell, shooting opposite the bars to make the nurse seem trapped on the other side of the turnstile, and capturing that moment where she just misses the train, a horror all commuters can identify with. Shot in gritty, guerrilla, late-70s fashion, it's beautiful and also totally dirty at the exact same time, just the way I like my Koch-era cult films.

Also a shout-out to the 2012 *Maniac* remake, which is gorgeously brutal and one of my favorites, but it doesn't officially make this list because that's Los Angeles, and who actually takes the subway in L.A.?

DRESSED TO KILL (1980)

I like to imagine a world in which Lustig and his film crew changed trains somewhere, probably Times Square, and crossed paths with Brian DePalma and his film crew, off to shoot *Dressed To Kill*, both released in the same year. Heck, while we're in Subway Fantasy Land, let's imagine Alan Parker's *Fame* crew crossing the platform for the local as John Cassavetes is down there blocking *Gloria* with wife Gena Rowlands. Look, 1980 was apparently a good year for shooting on the subway.

In *Dressed to Kill*, Nancy Allen is Liz Blake, a sex worker on the run from a tall, sunglass-sporting, razor-wielding blonde who she witnessed murder Angie Dickinson in an elevator. The blonde follows Liz into the Fulton Street station, which through the magic of filmmaking quickly becomes the curved platform of the S train in Times Square. Liz tries to blend in with a gang on the far end of the platform but gets way too close to them. (The first rule of subway-riding: respect your fellow passengers' personal space.) They start messing with her, and soon she's running not just from the blonde but from the gang as well.

On the train, she hops from subway car to subway car, the gang gaining ground. Flickering lights and POV shots heighten the tension as the camera spins around the cars, giving Liz nowhere to go but forward. The gang doesn't stop until she runs right into the black leather gloves of the blonde, in between the cars. Fortunately for Liz, Keith Gordon (playing Angie Dickinson's son) shows up with a can of homemade mace just in the nick of time. The gang scatters, the blonde is blinded, and Liz gets a sidekick for the rest of the film.

Lessons learned from *Dressed To Kill*? Don't walk between the subway cars lest you want to run into Michael Caine in a dress, and do carry your own mace so you don't have to depend on young nerd bros to save you.

Jacob's Ladder (1990)

One of the first scenes to kick off the phantasmagoric *Jacob's Ladder* takes place at the Bergen Street stop (right near my apartment). It's the mid-70s, and Tim Robbins' Jacob Singer wakes from a nightmarish flashback from his time in Vietnam to find he's fallen asleep on the C train. The car's pretty empty, save for a taciturn old woman and a homeless man with a scarf covering his face… and an alien tentacle between his legs. Jacob gets off at Bergen Street and tries to exit, but discovers the gates are all locked, and he's stuck inside the station. His only option? To cross the tracks and try to find a way out on the other side. And so, begins a very tense couple of minutes as Jacob lowers himself down onto the tracks and crosses them, managing to avoid the frightening third rail (the electrified one, so if you touch it, you're toast). Just as he's about to make it across, a train zooms in from the darkness. Jacob anxiously straddles the rails, trying to maintain his balance. At the last moment, he plunges to the side of the tracks, the train narrowly missing him. As it passes, strange Francis Bacon-esque figures stare down at him through the windows.

This scene hits a few raw nerves. First off, getting stuck in a subway station would totally suck, although personally, I'd rather spend the night in the station than attempt to cross the tracks. Second, is there actually enough space down there for one to duck and avoid being hit? You know, I'm good with never finding out. Third, dark figures in subway environments are scary as fuck and having them look down at you, emotionless, after you've narrowly escaped an oncoming train is next-level chilling. As intense as all this is, the movie only gets crazier from here.

Cloverfield (2008)

What do you do when a strange, skyscraper-size creature is running rampant around the city, taking out all of your national landmarks, but you've just got to get uptown to save the girl you love? High-tail it into the subway, I guess! The trains aren't running though, so *Cloverfield*'s group of 20-something partygoers needs to navigate the tunnels from Spring Street to 59th on foot in the dark. That's 60+ blocks, and of course the girls are wearing heels. (This movie is why I don't wear stilettos to NYC parties.) At least the power seems to be out, so the third rail isn't an issue. What is an issue, though, are the rats. Tons of them, and they're all running in the same direction. Via night vision, the partiers discover the rats are running from… GIANT SUBWAY SPIDERS! To be more specific, the rats are running from giant subway spiders that want to pounce on you and bite you and infect you with some venom that makes you burst into bloody pulp.

Talk about nightmare fuel. Thanks in part to the sound design, but mostly to the intrinsic terror of man-size spider/parasite creatures, this scene has scarred me. If the apocalypse comes to Manhattan, I'm sticking to the streets.

The Midnight Meat Train (2008)

Based on the short story by Clive Barker, *The Midnight Meat Train* is about a photographer (Bradley Cooper) who is obsessed with capturing New

York City's underbelly and is inspired to find even grittier subjects to shoot by his crush, hottie gallery-owner Brooke Shields. His midnight photo jaunts lead him right into the middle of a series of murders happening on train lines in the dead of the night: a butcher kills commuters and hangs them from the handrails like meat.

The movie is definitely shot in L.A., and the subway's color scheme doesn't pass for NYC at all, but we'll let all that slide because the film succeeds in prompting visceral reactions. In the way that you might yell at the Final Girl in a slasher movie, I found myself yelling at the screen: "Don't put on your headphones when it's only you and one weird dude on the other side of the train car!" And: "If you're going to listen to music, at least sit in a seat where you're facing him. Know where everyone is in the car at all times!" She didn't listen. They never do.

The movie builds to one of the most EPIC fight scenes I have ever seen take place on a subway car, wherein Bradley Cooper and Vinnie Jones battle it out with all sorts of stunts and acrobatics, among tons of dead, naked bodies hanging upside down like sides of beef. On long subway rides I've often gazed at the poles and imagined tossing myself around with the grace of a gymnast/pole dancer/martial arts expert and taking the Butcher out should I ever encounter him first-hand.

MIMIC (1997)

Guillermo del Toro's *Mimic* perfectly combines two of the things that frighten me most: the underground labyrinth of the subway system; and gigantic, flying, gene-enhanced un-killable cockroaches. (Even writing the word "cockroaches" freaks me out, like I'm summoning them to appear in my apartment by just saying their name.)

Let's back up. There's an epidemic that's killing the kids of New York City, and an entomologist (Mira Sorvino) discovers that by creating a form of super-cockroach, they can stop the virus that is infecting the kids because... science? Cut to three years later—Mira and her now-husband discover their bugs (which were supposed to die out once they did their job) are still alive and living large underneath Manhattan. Like, SUPER large. These roaches have grown six-feet tall and can trick us humans because they've developed a way to stand and look like us—with man-faces that break open to reveal their full cockroach selves! No no no no no no no no no.

In one of the most intense scenes, Mira and the gang are trapped inside an old broken subway car in the belly of the city as the creatures swarm, trying to get in, piercing the metal ceiling and walls with their stingers. *They can smell human blood!* The humans discover the only way they can trick them is to spread the gooey innards of a dead creature all over the car and their bodies, including their gaping wounds—which one character notes cannot be sanitary. This scene and movie have me giving subway critters a second glance—sure, they may be small now, but perhaps they're just a couple years away from evolving into your worst nightmare.

BONUS: *POSSESSION* (1981)

Perhaps no movie properly expresses my feelings about the subway better than *Possession*. In Andrzej Zulawski's criminally underseen psychosexual masterpiece, a married couple are on the brink of divorce—and insanity. The husband (Sam Neill) discovers his wife (Isabelle Adjani) is harboring a very dark secret in an apartment in another part of town. And while it's true the town in question is Berlin, not New York, I'm including it here because no other scene that I've come across properly encapsulates my anxieties about being in the subway more than *that* scene. If you've seen *Possession*, you know the one. And if not, no words I can write will ever do it justice, but if it helps, picture Adjani throwing her groceries against the subway station wall—eggs smashing, milk bursting—and flinging her body into the air, unleashing a manic dance of euphoria and hysteria, climaxing in some kind of demonic miscarriage that oozes out of every bodily orifice.

On the outside, to my fellow passengers, I may seem cool and collected, perhaps a little bored as I count the station stops. But if you ever see me on the subway, know that what's going on inside me is something far more extreme. What's going on inside me is what's happening to Isabelle Adjani in this scene.

What can I say? The New York City Subway takes you everywhere you want to go.

Horror Has Always Been a Smart Genre

by Carly Lane-Perry

If you've been following the news at any point over the last few years, you may have noticed a groundswell in the way horror movies are both covered and critiqued. "Smart horror is putting the fear into sequel-addicted Hollywood," declared The Guardian[1], in a piece from April 2018 timed to the release of *A Quiet Place* earlier that month. *Get Out (2017)* was praised for being "the smart horror gem we all deserve" in a review by Wired[2]. *Hereditary (2018)* was dubbed "the latest horror film to elevate the genre" by TIME[3].

But this is not a new phenomenon. What is new, relatively speaking, is the fact that "smart horror" has become the platitude mainstream outlets keep falling back on in an apparent attempt to lend unnecessary legitimacy to the long-standing genre and trying to distance these new movies from seemingly lesser contemporaries. Almost every time a relatively low-budget feature is released to strong box office returns and widespread acclaim, several critics are quick to declare that said film has ushered in a new era, one that will give rise to more intelligent horror—without actually taking the legacy behind these recent movies into account whatsoever. Horror has always been a smart genre, full of socially conscious messaging and subversively intelligent storytelling. The predecessors to films like *Hereditary* and *Get Out* can and do feel more dated in their themes to a modern audience, but that's only because, more often than not, they reflect the decade in which they were made, using the

---

1. https://www.theguardian.com/film/2018/apr/12/horror-quiet-place-get-out-hollywood
2. https://www.wired.com/2017/02/get-out-review/
3. https://time.com/5304199/hereditary-toni-collette/

lens of horror through which to address certain societal, political, racial, and patriarchal beliefs held at the time.

There's a reason the trope of the "Final Girl" has evolved so significantly over the last forty years. Part of her character is a manifestation of certain social mores, especially in regards to sexual activity and recreational drug use. While earlier versions of the Final Girl saw her refraining from the promiscuity and recklessness the rest of her friend group participated in, for fear she'd face the same terrifying fate, later variants were given more permission within the course of the story to express themselves more freely, without the threat of real consequence. These days, if the Final Girl has sex or smokes a joint, they're not necessarily acts that directly impact her chances of survival. If she makes it to the bitter end, she usually does so as a result of her own cunning, her clear-headedness in a time of deadly crisis, and her will to live.

The Final Girl isn't the only aspect of horror that we can look to as a direct reflection of the way in which the genre astutely addresses certain issues. Zombies have experienced a resurgence over the last few years thanks to the popularity of television shows like *The Walking Dead*, but it was George A. Romero's *Night of the Living Dead* in 1968 that invented the zombie genre as we know it today. After its initial release, Romero's first film was met with mostly negative reviews (Variety famously labeled it an "unrelieved orgy of sadism"), but in the fifty years since, it has gone on to become one of the most revered and celebrated additions to the zombie canon, not to mention the horror genre as a whole: in 1999, it was added to the Library of Congress' National Film Registry. Although Romero has gone on record several times to say that his casting of then-unknown stage actor Duane Jones was not intended to send a certain message[4] (his response was, simply, that Jones gave the best audition for a character who was originally written as white), a black man in a leading role in a '60s film was almost unheard of, to say nothing of the agency and the influence the script affords the character of Ben by positioning him as the movie's protagonist. He often assumes leadership and authority in making crucial choices that impact the safety of the rest of the group, who are all white. Romero may not have meant for his casting decision to change the overall significance of the film, especially in regards to its racial dynamics, but even without taking *Night of the Living Dead*'s affecting ending into account there are still important themes to be gleaned—all within a story

---

4. https://www.telegraph.co.uk/culture/film/10436738/George-A-Romero-Why-I-dont-like-The-Walking-Dead.html

that, at surface glance, appears to be just about a deadly zombie epidemic.

1973's *The Exorcist* was another example of a horror film that received mixed reviews when it first premiered, but later developed significant influence over not only the genre, but on the potential for horror to make waves during awards season. Though *Rolling Stone*'s Jon Landau initially decried it as "nothing more than a religious porn film," *The Exorcist* would go on to win the Golden Globe for Best Motion Picture, Drama, as well receive ten Oscar nominations, including for Best Picture, the first horror film ever to achieve that honor. Yet in a retrospective[5] published in 1998, BBC critic Mark Kermode indicated his reluctance to describe *The Exorcist* as an out-and-out horror film, saying, "Some people think it's an outright horror-fest, but I don't. It was written by a devout Catholic who hoped it would make people think positively about the existence of God." It's unclear why a movie that contains such scenes as Linda Blair's head rotating a full 180 degrees, an instance where words are literally carved into her character Regan's skin, and also a terrifying and lengthy exorcism for which the film is named isn't a "horror-fest."

Though twenty years have passed since Kermode's revisiting, his analysis highlights a problem that continues to persist across mainstream film criticism. Reviewers' reluctance to label horror films as exactly that are part of the reason so many misconceptions about the genre endure. A great horror flick can certainly posit existential questions about religion while still falling under the horror umbrella, and trying to disassociate certain titles by refusing to describe them as horror, or calling them simply "thrillers" instead (*The Hollywood Reporter*'s 2017 review of *It* is one such example[6]), only feeds into the mainstream belief that horror is a generally lowbrow genre, or the mistaken impression that it hasn't held a formative position within the landscape of film, even though history reveals plenty of evidence to the contrary.

When you consider the scope of horror not just domestically but within the foreign perspective, the evidence that the genre has always lent itself to astute, layered stories becomes even more apparent. *Suspiria*, released in 1977, has often been similarly referred to as a thriller or a suspense film by critics, when it would probably be more accurate to give it the horror moniker as well. On a visual level, with its saturated palette (in fact, *Suspiria* was one of the last films to be released in Technicolor),

---

5. https://books.google.com/books?id=jLiUKCPQWj8C&printsec=frontcover&source=kp_read_button%22%20%5Cl%20%22v=onepage&q&f=false#v=onepage&q&f=false

6. https://www.hollywoodreporter.com/review/it-review-1035328

the setting almost appears too bright to serve as the backdrop to one of the most supernaturally arresting foreign horror films in history. Yet director and co-writer Dario Argento paired these vivid colors with the supernatural allure of the witches who run (and rule) the prestigious Tanz Dance Academy to create plenty of thrilling—and horrifying—moments. Although the film itself is somewhat scant on overall plot, *Suspiria's* aesthetic is one that continues to be praised and is a significant part of what has led to its achievement of cult status. It was a horror movie that pushed the boundaries of what horror necessarily needed to visually fit into in order to be commercially successful, and its longevity has even led to a 2018 remake by another Italian filmmaker, Luca Guadagnino. His version doesn't try to mimic what made the original so unique as much as it enriches the bones of an already compelling story.

Fast-forwarding to the last twenty years, many of the horror films that continue to be brought up time and time again are the ones that have set their own unique precedents within the genre. When director Wes Craven and writer Kevin Williamson teamed up for the release of 1996's *Scream*, it was a turning point. With a script that lovingly lampooned the tropes of previous horror franchises (including a lengthy sequence on the unwritten but relied-upon "rules" of such films as John Carpenter's *Halloween* [1978]) and the casting of big-name actors at the time like Drew Barrymore and Courteney Cox, *Scream* managed to revitalize a genre that had stalled in recent years, sparking a new demand for slasher films that paired witty dialogue and self-aware commentary with young actors on the rise. Its success would induce several other movies made in a similar vein, including *I Know What You Did Last Summer* (1997) and *Urban Legend* (1998), but *Scream* was arguably a benchmark all its own, and the fact that it continues to be dissected and discussed in equal measure makes the case for why it should be considered yet another archetype for smart, groundbreaking horror.

Films that popularized or essentially legitimized a specific subgenre should also not be discounted from the ongoing discourse about the kinds of movies that have elevated horror as a whole. *The Blair Witch Project* may have seen its fair share of parodies after it was released in 1999, but without its clever implementation of the "found-footage technique," subsequent popular horror franchises like *Paranormal Activity* (2007) and *Cloverfield* (2008) would have never come to pass. *The Blair Witch Project* was a perfect example of the type of low-budget, high-returns horror film that critics tend to praise now, though interestingly enough, audience reactions were initially mixed when the film first premiered. Its mostly improvised script and untried cinematography (the only cameras used were wielded by the actors themselves) gave the film a surprising believability, and it was even promoted via the Internet as being recovered documentary footage rather than a work of fiction. *The Blair Witch Project* is smart horror not only for its innovation, but for its infused sense of realism. It was a movie that dared to try something new and kickstarted an entire subcategory within the genre as a result.

In some ways, we also have *The Blair Witch Project* to thank for indirectly spearheading another popular and equally brilliant horror film. Director James Wan and writer Leigh Whannell were inspired to self-finance and make 2004's *Saw* together after witnessing the success of that preceding project. While *Saw* spawned a franchise all its own, and several of those subsequent sequels have been subpar, there's no denying that the first installment is pure brilliance, psychological horror combined with just the right amount of stomach-churning gore to create a formula for success. Over the years, however, the *Saw* franchise has come to be remembered more for its decimating death traps than the twisted cerebral mind games that equally serve to elevate the story's tension. In the legacy of the horror canon, *Saw*'s intelligence shouldn't be omitted just because it has a high body count; if anything, its endurance serves as proof that the two can co-exist simultaneously and, ultimately, evolve the genre past what it once was.

The label of "smart horror" doesn't just apply to more recent movies, as any diehard fan can attest. Even in examining some of horror's most popular films, we've only just scratched the surface of the genre. As the popularity of horror continues to rise, however, more and more reviewers are giving a second look to something that they may have once overlooked or previously dismissed as lowbrow, campy, or even trashy. It's encouraging to see horror emerging into a more accepted place in mainstream criticism, but it's also a reminder that it hasn't always been appreciated or acknowledged for not only its contributions across the realm of cinema but also its social commentary—incisive, profound, and above all, smart. While horror continues to carve out a unique place for itself, we should never forget the progress it's already achieved and the lessons we've already learned from some of the most iconic and terrifying stories ever made.

Taking the 'Ick' out of Ichthyology: Gender in the *Creature from the Black Lagoon* Trilogy

by Heather Hendershot

I SHOULD OPEN BY SAYING that I realize my title is a bit silly. But it's not frivolous: what I'm pointing to with my "ick" reference is a double-sided revulsion explored throughout the *Creature From the Black Lagoon* trilogy. First, there is the revulsion expressed toward the monster, as a non-human but human-like being. It is telling that he is actually referred to most often in the films themselves not as "the Creature" but as the "Gill-Man." Half fish and half man, it is in part this in-between-ness that makes him so repulsive to those who fear him; as with so many monsters, his creepiness lies in this border confusion. (Other exemplary monsters are dead/undead, man/wolf, man/fly…you see what I mean.) At the same time, the one hundred percent human men of the series express revulsion toward a different kind of other: the independent woman.

The following pages chart the progression I see throughout the *Creature* films, in which woman and Creature are aligned, separated, and re-aligned in interesting ways, and, ultimately, doomed by a repressive, sexist and racist patriarchal society. To be clear, although the films themselves do not consistently and collectively speak from a pro-liberation standpoint, they do overtly recognize the oppression that they picture, drawing it to our attention. And by the time we get to the third installment of the series, *The Creature Walks Among Us* (John Sherwood, 1956), the worldview expressed is so bleak that I believe we can only see the film as truly radical. I will discuss all three pictures, with a particular focus on the third. First, however, it will be helpful to provide some background context.

Critical analysis of horror films took root in academia following the publication of Robin Wood and Richard Lippes' *The American Nightmare* in 1979.[1] Wood would quickly become the preeminent critic of American horror films, advancing an influential theory that the politically progressive horror film features a monster configured as an Other, and that this Other expresses that which bourgeois patriarchal capitalism most fears: female power, bisexuality, infantile sexuality—in brief, difference. Wood was most interested in radical horror films of the 1970s such as *The Texas Chainsaw Massacre* (Tobe Hooper, 1974), *The Last House on the Left* (Wes Craven, 1972), *The Hills Have Eyes* (Wes Craven, 1977), *It's Alive!* (Larry Cohen, 1974), *God Told Me To* (Larry Cohen, 1976), and *Dawn of the Dead* (George A. Romero, 1978), films he discusses in detail in his classic book *Hollywood from Vietnam to Reagan*.[2]

Wood was dubious about any film that represented monsters as pure evil, since it was precisely the complexity of the monster and its status as a creation of (or projection of the anxieties of) putatively normal people that made it politically interesting. The best, most progressive horror films question the very idea of normality, he contended, often portraying "normal" people as more monstrous than the monsters that threaten them. This was true not only of much of 1970s horror but also of the classic Universal films of the 1930s such as *Frankenstein* (James Whale, 1931) and *Bride of Frankenstein* (James Whale, 1935).

It is telling that Wood skips from the thirties to the seventies. While there is little doubt that he would have recognized a few subversive moments in this interim period (in the films of William Castle, for example), it is also true that the complex, progressive portrayal of monsters receded during this interregnum, when many film monsters were faceless space invaders, often obvious Communist stand-ins. It is helpful to add here that the 1950s were a peak moment for not only horror but also science fiction, and that the two were often fused. While we can devise a taxonomic structure to delineate the differences between horror and science fiction (the former is more likely to embrace the supernatural than the latter, for example), sorting out whether a film is "really" horror or science fiction is often

---

1. Robin Wood and Richard Lippe, eds. *American Nightmare: Essays on the Horror Film* (Toronto: Festival of Festivals, 1979).

2. Robin Wood, *Hollywood from Vietnam to Reagan* (New York: Columbia University Press, 1985).

not a very productive exercise, especially when tackling the films of the fifties, which were often marketed interchangeably as horror and science fiction. Both were extremely popular market categories, and marketers targeted viewers who were looking to be thrilled and scared by monsters in general, whether concocted in laboratories, sent from Mars, or blasted loose from beneath the ocean floor.

The vast majority of these Cold War horror/sci-fi monsters lacked the subtlety that would enable viewers to feel sympathy for them. For every big budget smart film like *The Day the Earth Stood Still* (Robert Wise, 1951), or small budget clever film like *The Wasp Woman* (Roger Corman, 1959), there were hundreds of clunkers like *Teenagers from Outer Space* (Tom Graeff, 1959), great fun if you are in a *Mystery Science Theater 3000* frame of mind, but not offering deep insights on the motivations of alien invaders (who in this case were, clearly, actually lobsters!).

In any case, Wood is spot-on in pointing to *the provocation of empathy for those who are different* as one of the most politically radical and satisfying things that a horror film can offer, and if most fifties film offered little on this front where monsters were concerned, it is worth pointing out that the human leads also tended to be a bit thin in these pictures. The men were often engineers or scientists, the women wives or girlfriends. The men solved the problem of alien/monster invasion, often with hefty support from the US military. The women got carried away by the monsters and needed to be rescued.

"Carried away" held a clear implication of intended sexual violence, and getting to the women "on time" meant before they were murdered but also before they were raped. Whether the monster was coded specifically as a racial other or more vaguely as simply a monstrous other, the fear of miscegenation—of inappropriate, border-crossing sex—was powerfully present. Not every nine-year-old viewer necessarily understood all of this, and the censorship standards of the time meant that the threat of sexual violence generally had to be more implied than directly stated, but to deny the sexual threat of the 1950s monster is to operate from a position of willful ignorance. The films of this era are replete with images of monsters carrying women in their arms, like a groom carrying his bride over the threshold, except that the women are passed out, draped backwards, and likely to be in a shape-hugging bathing suit or conveniently ripped, thin garment. Even Robbie the Robot is pictured on the *Forbidden Planet* (Fred M. Wilcox, 1956) poster with a sexpot in his arms, which is patently ridiculous in light of the fact that Robbie was not only utterly lacking in sexual aggressivity but also one of the more benign and likeable characters in the film. But the threat of violation was what sold tickets, so the film's poster had to hint at sexual assault.

In sum, fifties horror films were frequently normative in their politics—showing the id erupt in the form of a monster which would then be suppressed by a normalizing superego in human form. The normalization might be conservative, but representing the eruption itself could have progressive potential. *Forbidden Planet*, for example, showed a monster created by human anger, anxiety, and incestuous desire. This was a "monster from the id," the film's heroes exclaimed. It had to be destroyed, but the monstrosity of human nature had been laid bare by the monster's very existence. Across the board, as Margaret Tarratt has argued, the 1950s monsters from the id would have to be quashed by human superego forces.[3] Tarratt's monster-as-id is in many ways just another version of Wood's monstrous Other, but Tarratt's id-monster is firmly contained, while Wood's id-monster is more transgressive in its implications. Both point to the same basic idea: American horror films express a fear of dangerous sexuality.

On the surface, the *Creature* trilogy offers yet another clear example of the monstrous id formulation. And yet, the series also takes pains to point to the monstrosity of *human* masculinity, and by the third film it is clear that it is the human characters who are most sexually dangerous.

The Creature from the Black Lagoon (Jack Arnold, 1954) features a female lead who initially seems fairly independent and capable. Kay is the sidekick of our hero, the scientist David, and she is employed by the oceanographic institute run by the villainous Mark. Her job is ambiguous. At first we guess she may be a scientist, but there are other moments when we might reasonably assume that she is a secretary. She is, at the very least, a helpmate to David. Early in the film, she gives him a shoulder to lean on as he takes off his flippers following a deep dive. Then she drives their boat back to shore, which is delightfully shocking; when a man is available to drive in almost any movie, he grabs the wheel. Women only drive when there is no man around, and there is a good chance that a woman driver means trouble. (Consider the over-sexed hellraiser Dorothy Malone in *Written on the Wind* [Douglas Sirk, 1956]).

Shortly after Kay has displayed her competence piloting a skiff, she joins the men in examining a recently discovered fossilized claw from

---

3. Margaret Tarratt, "Monsters from the Id" in Barry Keith Grant, ed. *Film Genre Reader II* (Austin: University of Texas Press, 1995), 330–349.

some kind of evolutionary abomination—a relative of our titular Creature, of course. At this point, she seems like part of the team, asking questions and exhibiting interest. ("How do you account for the structure of the fingers, obviously for land use?") But it is David who most strongly exerts his scientific curiosity, while Mark reveals his cutthroat instincts. David wants to return to the Amazon for more fossils to study; Mark hopes the institute can make money on any curiosities they can discover. One must intuit that Kay is a "good guy," as she is partnered with David. But she has no particular opinions to express here.

Upon arriving in the Amazon, a few innocent victims of the Creature are found, and the men's instinct is to protect Kay from seeing their corpses. Once they decide to go up to a mysterious lagoon to pursue more artifacts, speculation is offered that, "going into unexplored territory with a woman" is risky but Kay says she's not afraid, and Mark adds that Kay is "able to take care of herself." The men pursue their work, while Kay takes a swim…without even getting permission first. She wears a one-piece that star Julie Adams later described as a little racy for the time, as it was cropped up a bit over the thighs in the front. It was specially built for the film and was murder to get in and out of, especially given that it was bright white, and Adams had been painted with body make-up. Rigid vertical piping runs through the center of each breast, drawing attention to the star's bosom, even as her cleavage remains safely encased. The swimwear clearly has a serious infrastructure, designed to amplify Kay's physique.

One of the most famous sequences in horror film history ensues, as Kay swims on the surface with sensuous vigor, unaware that the Creature swims on his back beneath her, expressing sadness and longing. Introduced as both coworker and girlfriend to David, Kay has by now been reduced to her status as object of desire—desire of David, Mark, and now the monster. David is the "victor," insofar as she has already chosen him. Yet Mark still desires her, and the Creature is a newly arrived rival for her affections. Strikingly, Mark tries to kill the Gill-Man almost immediately, and clearly cares for little more than power and monetary gain, while the sad Creature secretly swimming beneath his would-be lover is patently more sympathetic than Mark up on the surface. The commentary on what it means to be human is obviously compelling, in the best Robin Wood tradition: David may be the more suitable love interest for Kay, but the Creature cannot fail to elicit our sympathy, even as the ruthless Mark can elicit nothing but contempt from any viewer who values compassion and intellectual curiosity. What is lost here, though, is the possibility of Kay conveying her own desire (intellectual, sexual, or otherwise) beyond her plot function as The Love Interest. If she does exhibit desire following the swimming scene (which we could legitimately read as auto-erotic), it is the desire to function as a relationship manager, making peace between rival beaus.

One crucial exchange late in the film seals my reading. The Gill-Man has been captured and is being held in a tank on the ship. As the Creature maneuvers to escape, Dr. Thompson (played by the ever competent genre actor Whit Bissell) engages in an interesting conversation with Kay.

> Thompson: You're worried about what's happened between Mark and David. But once you admit the simple fact that you're in love, which you have, then it becomes a good idea to be the scientist about it.
>
> Kay: It's not as easy as that.
>
> Thompson: Why not?
>
> Kay: Well, if it weren't for Mark Williams I wouldn't have my work, or even a job.
>
> Thompson: True, he helped you with your training and gave you a job. But he needed you just as much as you needed him.
>
> Kay: You're over-simplifying.
>
> Thompson: You've more than repaid him many times over. Why, a good part of his present position at the Institute is due to your valuable research. And another thing—

At this point, the two are interrupted by the escaping Creature. Indeed, throughout the scene the importance of the dialogue is undercut by cutaways to the Creature edging closer to escaping from his tank. It is arguably Kay's most interesting moment; we learn that she has done valuable research, and that she is trapped in this love triangle largely because she feels guilty walking out on the man who jumpstarted her education and gave her a good job. At the same time, the dialogue is positioned as filler, as suspense builds relentlessly regarding the Creature's next move.

Further, advised by a man to be logical and scientific (to be rational and stop fretting about the problems between the two men), Kay responds with an insistence upon feeling emotional (guilty) instead. Thompson is basically telling her to act more like a man, and she refuses. From here on, Kay's job in the film is mostly to scream, be abducted, and be rescued—standard stuff for a female lead in a 1950s horror movie (and later, of course). Given how the film tilts toward science fiction, one intuits that Kay's role as scientist—or at least apprentice—should be relevant to understanding her function in the film, yet this relevance is never allowed to play itself out.

Still, at least like David she harbors no animus toward the Gill-Man. She's afraid of him, yet she does not perceive him as deliberately malevolent. This is one of the most powerful elements of the first film in the series: the good guys recognize the Gill-Man as acting according to his animal nature, and they realize that it is *they* who have invaded *his* territory. From his perspective, it is the humans who are monsters, a notion driven home by Mark's bloodlust to destroy him. The Creature kills like any animal in the wild would to defend itself, but Mark kills out of sadistic machismo. The film conveys this notion over and over again, and this aspect of it can only be seen as progressive.[4] Ultimately, *The Creature from the Black Lagoon* offers a strong critique of toxic masculinity, valuing the intelligent and compassionate man over the anti-intellectual and violent man. Where it stops short is in saying anything interesting about the ways a *woman* might play a different role in this male-dominated world.

It is to some extent a relief, then, when the female lead of the next film, Miss Helen Dobson, is introduced to us as an aspiring ichthyologist. In *Revenge of the Creature* (Jack Arnold, 1955), the Gill-Man has been rescued and brought to a nautical theme park in Florida, where he will be both exhibited to tourists and studied by scientists. Helen is there to participate in the study, to gather material for her master's thesis. She is immediately paired with Dr. Clete Ferguson, played by the barely competent and vaguely seedy John Agar. Taking a break from work, they

---

4. The counter example is the unmotivated killing of two native assistants early in the film, which is pure treachery. The creature also kills two Amazonian natives later on the boat. These dramatic scenes are patently designed to exploit 3D technology, to thrill viewers; the fact that we are not meant to feel anything for these victims is patently racist.

have an exchange that I find absolutely astonishing by the standards of 1950s horror/sci-fi:

> Helen: It's nice to get away, lie in the sun, be like other people.
>
> Clete: Strange talk coming from a dedicated scientist. Have you forgotten your mission in life? I'll be leaving soon. I'm going to miss you.
>
> Helen: You know, sometimes I wonder how I ever got started on all this…science, fish, ichthyology. Where will it all lead me? As a person, I mean. Most of the kids I went to undergraduate school with are already married and have children.
>
> Clete: Is that what you want?
>
> Helen: I don't know. I just don't know.
>
> Clete: But surely you must—
>
> Helen: —but what do *you* want?
>
> Clete: Well, it's different with me. I'm a man. I don't have to make a choice.
>
> Helen: But I do?
>
> Clete: It's tough on you gals. I'm not saying it's right or wrong. It's just a fact.
>
> Helen: Doesn't seem right.
>
> Clete: But you haven't told me what you want. What you want most I mean. I'd like to know before I leave. You've become important to me.
>
> Helen: Very?
>
> Clete: Uh-huh.

At this point, Clete leans in for a smooch, with Helen receptive, but they are immediately interrupted by Helen's playful dog.

Now, there are obviously melodramas of this era that deal much more extensively with the dual crises of female desire and entrapment—Douglas Sirk's *All that Heaven Allows* (1955) being a particularly pointed example—but Clete's acknowledgment that women must choose marriage or family, and Helen's response that this seems unfair, is pretty heady stuff for a modestly budgeted 1950s genre picture. (Granted, it's shot in 3D, so it's hardly a cheap picture, but let's just say that no money was wasted on interesting sets, costumes, locations, or acting talent.) It's sad that Clete won't explicitly take a stand on whether the fact that women must choose between career and family is right or wrong, yet his own comfort with the fact that he does not have to make the choice himself implies that he's actually quite comfortable with the whole system. Indeed, by the end of the scene he is clear that not only must Helen choose, she must choose *soon*, before he leaves town. He's not really listening to her, it turns out, which is in keeping with what we know of his character. Still, the fact that this exchange on inequality even happens is shocking.

Regrettably, Helen—like Kay—is soon reduced to her to-be-rescued function. She gets a chance to show off her figure in a carefully managed (sexy but not *too* sexy) shower scene, and her dog is murdered by the Creature. At the end of the day, it is a thankless role, and Helen's ichthyological skill set is left largely untapped. Although Helen's role as scientist is more front and center than Kay's, she notably uses her scientific knowledge for *evil*. In *Revenge*, the Creature is not only imprisoned in a tank, but Helen and Clete regularly enter the tank to "train" him, using a cattle prod for negative reinforcement. There are other fish in the tank, but he is chained to the floor so that he does not harm them, or escape from the tank. He is allowed to eat dead fish from a metal basket. There is no convincing pretense of scientific inquiry here: the Creature is enslaved, and this is torture. At one point, as he consumes the meal his captors have provided him, Helen uncharitably observes, "He's not much on table manners is he?" Unforgivably, the line is delivered as a light joke.

It is perhaps easier to feel empathy for the Creature in this installment of the series than in the first one, because none of the human characters are likely to elicit sympathy: surrounded by immoral characters, this amoral character comes closest to occupying the high ground. At the same time, if I am to be honest, I do find the repeated scenes of Helen looking through the porthole into the tank and the Creature looking back out at her—rarely at the same time, it's more as if they are stealing glances at each other—to be poignant. The script does not make the point explicit, but the visuals do point to each as trapped in his or her world.[5]

All in all, there is a lot of potential in the second film, in light of the fact that the Creature has been captured and tortured, and is held in a facility that is less a scientific laboratory than a circus side show where people can pay to gaze at the Gill-Man like a freakish curiosity. (I find myself recalling the monster enchained in the dungeon in *Bride of Frankenstein*, as the crowd howls at him through the bars above.) The set-up seems amenable to Robin Wood's definition of the progressive horror film, and yet it doesn't follow through. In the first film, the ethical battle between Mark and David made clear that harming the Creature was wrong. Yet Clete exhibits neither Mark's animosity toward the Creature nor David's kindness.[6] *Revenge* is disinterested in condemning the Creature's torment. Clete and Helen never doubt the validity of their tortuous experiments. In fact, Helen is saved at the end of the film because Clete shouts "stop!," and the cattle prod training kicks in, making the Creature drop Helen, as if succumbing to Pavlovian instinct. Ultimately, the moral of the film resonates with Clete's cowardly acknowledgment that men don't have to make the choices that women make. Torturing the Gill-Man with a cattle prod is neither right nor wrong in this film: it's just a fact.

The Gill-Man and Helen may be in a similar bind in some ways, caught in circumstances beyond their control, but they will never come to terms with those parallel circumstances. Indeed, Helen will take advantage of being higher on the totem pole by teaming up with the men who oppress her to oppress someone with even less power. The racial subtext that underpins so many monster movies—the notion that repulsive creatures, half-breeds, and aliens live to steal "our women"—is clearly played out in the scenario of Helen, the would-be scientist forced to choose between career and family, turning on the enchained primitive (explicitly understood as lower on the evolutionary chain than our white heroes), a primitive who, true to stereotypical form, conveys immediate sexual interest in her as soon as he is freed from his chains. For of course,

---

5. *The Shape of Water* (Guillermo del Toro, 2017) obviously takes inspiration from the *Creature* trilogy, and it is perhaps the second film in the series that offers the most direct inspiration. *Water* feels like a remake unveiling the unexplored potential of *Revenge*.

6. At the end of the film, the creature has been shot, but David prevents him from being killed and instead allows him to get away. Yes, this enables the possibility of a sequel, but it also is consistent with David's reluctance to harm the creature except in self-defense.

he inevitably escapes, makes off with Helen, is forced to release her, and swims away, wounded but not dead, leaving open the option of a third film.

This brings me at last to the jewel in the crown of the series, *The Creature Walks Among Us* (John Sherwood, 1956). To be clear, the first film is the tightest—most suspenseful, most skillfully acted, most crowd-pleasing, and most aesthetically impressive. By most criteria, it would be judged "the best." But I believe the third film is ultimately the most interesting, and the most progressive. In fact, I would go far as to say that it is one of the most politically radical horror pictures of the 1950s.

The film opens with our female lead, Mrs. Marcia Barton, driving fast with Dr. Barton beside her. In most films, fast driving indicates a loose woman, but it turns out that Marcia Barton is trapped and bored, but not promiscuous; she is looking for stimulation, but not stimulation of a carnal nature. Marcia and her husband head out to the sea to capture the Creature, along with Dr. Morgan (our hero and would-be romantic lead), a few other scientists and technicians, and Grant, who is the expedition guide but spends most of the film trying to corner and violate Marcia.

Within moments, Marcia is shooting at sharks, to save a school of dolphins. The film frames this as benevolent, though that point is of course debatable. As a plot point, it helps to introduce the film's species-ism. Mammals are at the top, and those "lower" on the evolutionary chain are understood as more barbaric. Man's goal is to reach the stars, viewers are told several times, but if he slips too far in the other direction, he will fall into the jungle. In this context, a human murdering a shark is somehow superior to a shark trying to get its dinner. Aside from showing that Marcia is to be admired, the film's interest in the hierarchy of species helps introduce the notion that Dr. Barton is an unhinged, mad scientist type. His objective in capturing the Creature is to push him from his hybrid half-fish, half-human status into a fully human creature. He wants to play God, in other words. Dr. Morgan counters, "I disagree. We can learn from nature, help nature. We can make this earth a happier place by helping nature select what's best in us. And when man's ready, mentally, physically, we'll get to outer space. But doctor, there's no shortcut. You can't bypass nature." Barton dismisses this kind of thinking as small. He is, in short, a lunatic.

Barton is also a sadistic husband who berates his wife and accuses her of infidelity. Amazingly, she keeps pushing back, insisting, for example, on going diving with Morgan and Grant. This deep-sea swim enables a showcase scene of underwater photography, and, of course, plenty of footage of her in a bathing suit. Yet unlike in the first film, the swimsuit here is made of heavy material with cuffed edging, looking less like a bathing beauty costume than an abbreviated sweater. She goes too deep and gets what they call "deep diving sickness" (or "raptures of the deep"), like being drunk on pressure instead of champagne, as Marcia puts it. This leads her into a bit of loopy auto-erotic swimming designed for our viewing pleasure. Yet what is remarkable is that the Creature is present, yet ignores her. Morgan and Grant also do not watch. No one is *interested* in this sensuous display. Given how often Marcia is subjected to masculine violence (she narrowly escapes being raped by her husband in a later scene), this solitary deep-water swim must be a kind of respite for her.

Finally, Morgan rescues her, as she attempts to discard her breathing apparatus. Back on board, an odd conversation follows.

> Marcia: I'm sorry I made so much trouble.
>
> Morgan: You're a very brave woman. You shouldn't take such chances.
>
> Marcia: You know, taking chances isn't just a man's privilege.
>
> Morgan: Trying to kill oneself isn't either.
>
> Marcia: You take risks.
>
> Morgan: I take calculated risks for a purpose. What are *you* trying to prove?
>
> Marcia: I should have known. You're a scientist. You need proof. You'd never take anyone's word for anything.
>
> Morgan: I deserved that. Forgive me. If there's anything I can do…
>
> Marcia: No, there's nothing anyone can do. Ten years ago, when I was 17, when Dr.Barton married me, I…I'm really feeling sorry for myself now, aren't I? Look, I've managed to

learn a few things. At least I know what the world undersea looks like. It can be very beautiful.

One feels for Marcia, because no one else has been interested in actually talking to her. And Morgan is simply being nice, without making romantic overtures. He's smart, but also pretty dull. Yet he's the only patently decent man around. Grant, conversely, has already wrapped his arms around Marcia in the guise of adjusting her breathing apparatus, and shortly after this scene with Morgan, Grant will pin her against the wall in a narrow corridor. He has also referred to Marcia as one of her husband's "possessions," in an effort to demean her. His sole objective in the film is to rape her. The terror of this situation is writ large by the film; it is a stark contrast to the typical 1950s representation of rape, which could be boiled down to she-was-asking-for-it.[7]

Having deposited Marcia on the boat, the men go out and capture the Creature. In the course of this action, the Creature is terribly burned, and irreparable damage is done to his gills. The science is ludicrous, but the bottom line is that following a tracheotomy, the men manage to activate the Creature's vestigial lungs (not farfetched insofar as we've seen him on land; he is amphibious). His genetic structure has changed, he is no longer a fish, and he is changing to become more and more like a man. Because of his burns, he has been wrapped up like a mummy, and when the bandages are removed from his face, his iconic, giant fish eyes have disappeared. He now has human eyes. The webbing on his hands is reduced, and he has digits with fingernails instead of claws. He has lost his scales and dorsal fins; he now has skin, though it remains thick and clammy in appearance. It is the close-up of his face that is most striking. For now that he is a man, we can read him not as a metaphorical person of color (as the monstrous other is in so many horror films) but, more simply, as a person of color. His large lips and flattened nose, which before indicated he was a fish, now indicate that he is black. The notion that his human nature is tricky, that he is still close to "the jungle" and may revert to the violence of the jungle would seem to seal my reading—and would also seem to confirm the film's white supremacy. But then the film goes farther.

Escaping from his room, the Creature bursts in upon Grant, who is making his first full-fledged attempt to rape Marcia. She cries out to Grant

---

7. See for example the inappropriately sexy teacher in *Blackboard Jungle* (Richard Brooks, 1955), who self-indulgently hikes up her skirt to adjust her stocking, and then later, as a matter of course, is sexually assaulted.

"please, let me go!" as the Creature breaks through the door, breaking up the clinch. Marcia falls on the couch and looks up in terror. It is exactly the moment when the monster makes off with the screaming woman—in every other horror movie. But here, the Creature sees her but has no interest in her whatsoever. Instead, he jumps overboard, almost drowns (no gills), and Dr. Morgan rescues him, risking his own life as he convinces the Creature to share a breathing tube with him. It is in this sequence that it is finally confirmed that even though the movie's jungle-versus-the-stars evolutionary discourse is a bit dodgy, the film's stance is radical in three ways.

First, the Creature is better than most of the people in the film, in large part because he is neither violent nor specifically interested in harming women. Second, he may be visually coded as a person of color, but he has no interest in taking "our" white women, unlike virtually every other movie monster of this period; this disinterest destabilizes the psychosis of the white terror of black sexuality that is a rolling subtext of so many monster movies. And third, the scene reveals that Morgan is the moral center of the film; he endangers himself to save the Creature. The rescue is surprising because it is not imperative. That is, the plot does not need the monster to live; there's nothing at stake in practical terms. There would be no real repercussions if he died. Morgan saves him because he feels a moral obligation to save the life of another man, regardless of the fact that that man is radically "other," not just a monster but also a monster coded as African American. In other words, this sequence reveals the film's moral compass. In this world, a white man would give his life to save a black man, because that's what humans should do for each other. It's not deep philosophy, but it's the stuff we expect of "social problem" films like *To Kill a Mockingbird* (Robert Mulligan, 1962) or *Crossfire* (Edward Dmytryk, 1947), not the stuff we expect of low-rent genre pictures.

This is not to say that *The Creature Walks Among Us* can be reduced to a progressive racial allegory. Indeed, Dr. Morgan's insistence that evolution means progress and progress means displacing instinct for more civilized interaction clearly has a backward, racialized motivation. Pushing back against Dr. Barton's insistence that the transformed Creature is a new species, for example, Morgan says, "We only changed the skin, doctor, not the animal. But we can bring out the best or worst in any living thing…. We all stand between the jungle and the stars, at a crossroads. I think we better discover what brings out the best in humankind, and what brings out the worst. Because it's the stars, or the jungle." The insistence that the jungle is "the worst" is cringe-worthy, to say the least.

To his credit, though, Morgan insists that the transformed Creature responds appropriately to pain, or to kindness. If he is treated kindly, he will not be violent. One of Morgan's final observations at the end of the film is that the Creature only killed in self-defense, and this obvious point forces us to look back and realize something shocking that we may have missed: this is a horror movie in which the monster only kills twice, targeting an animal predator that attacked him without provocation and the sadistic man who tortured him and is responsible for his unwanted transformation. This so-called monster has performed no monstrous acts, but he has nonetheless been hunted, burned, genetically modified, imprisoned, and shot. This fact, coupled with Morgan's sympathy and his notion that this monster is actually very much like a human, neither inherently good nor evil but, rather, responding appropriately to those around him, is radical in the context of horror film history. Consider, by contrast, the relentless torture of the Frankenstein creature throughout a number of *Frankenstein* films. Viewers are often meant to feel sorry for him, but few characters in the films feel sympathy for him.

Alas, after Morgan's rescue, the Creature must endure further indignities. He is moved to Sausalito, CA, and as he exits the windowless transport van, dressed in shapeless oversized clothing, he looks like a prisoner. Three men with cowboy hats, two of them holding rifles, await him menacingly right outside the van. Anyone paying attention to the news at the time would have seen many images of southern Blacks being stuffed into paddy wagons by white men with guns. One can only think of southern sheriffs at this point, regardless of the West Coast location. The Creature is put into a large, electrified outdoor cage with barbed wire. As the humans a few feet away in the house sort through their jealousies and pathologies, the Creature stares at a lagoon, just out of reach outside of the cage. He doesn't want to kill or rape. He just wants to get back in the water. Adding to the dramatic tension, Marcia goes for a swim to get away from her pathological husband, only to be followed by Grant, who clearly intends to assault her again. The attack is preempted when a mountain lion enters the Creature's cage—the aforementioned predator, killed by the Creature. But this plot point is less interesting than the Creature watching the human predator and his prey in the lagoon, with a look of longing that conveys not that he is part of a love triangle (à la Dracula/Jonathan/Mina, a more typical set up), but that he simply wants to be free to return to the water.

The Creature finally breaks free from his captors and is shot by one of the rifle-wielding southern sheriff types. Grant and Dr. Barton are killed along the way, and the implication is that it is their own fault, because they are treacherous sadists incapable of impulse control. We are left with the possibility that the widowed Marcia and the ever-gracious and stoic Morgan will perhaps pursue a relationship in the future, but there is no clichéd final clinch. Further, running counter to the final pairing of the couple that is the familiar fade-to-black of so many films, Marcia and Morgan's final, restrained farewell—a romantic handshake (seriously!)—does not close out the film. Instead, the closing shot is of the Creature, who rises over the ridge of a sand dune. He's been shot, so he is unsteady, but he staggers toward the sea. The clear implication is that in returning to his home, he is committing suicide.

The scene is almost unbelievable. The Creature does not kill himself because of unrequited love (think of the finale of *King Kong* [Merian C. Cooper, 1933]: "It was beauty killed the beast.") He does not kill himself because he is too monstrous to exist in this world, which would be a different kind of romantic ending, like the Frankenstein monster drifting away on a glacier at the end of Shelley's novel. He does not kill himself because he's going to die anyway; there is no clear indication that the gunshot wounds are fatal. He kills himself because the ocean is where he wants to be, but not because he "belongs" there away from the "civilized" folks on land. These humans have, after all, shown themselves to be worthless. Ultimately, the Creature goes in the ocean because it is *his desire* to do so. In this desire, he is like Kay and Marcia, who also took elicit swims for which they were ultimately punished. Unless you are a white man in the *Creature* films, you just can't win. You can only die trying.

Adolescence and Horror

A Cure For Your Disco Problems

by Debbie Rochon

THE 1970S WERE A WONDERFUL TIME to be a serial killer. No DNA technology, no cell phones pinging towers, very few CCV cameras to capture your depraved likeness. You could be the lowest form of humanity and get away with it. Many did. Body counts were high and the desecration of the, mostly, female form was of the lowest, degraded brutality a person could unleash upon a victim. Yes, these were the glory days for the dregs of society.

What came out of this era could be, arguably, some of the best art from all disciplines; music, film, painting and writing. Certainly, the horror film benefited from this raw time period. Some of the most disturbing, original and realistic horror flicks came from the 1970s, including *The Texas Chain Saw Massacre* (1974), *The Hills Have Eyes* (1977), *Don't Look Now* (1973), *Last House on the Left* (1972), and *Tourist Trap* (1979). Cult movies also had their antiheros trying to navigate their way through the darkness of the 1970s. *Mad Max* (1979), *Taxi Driver* (1976) and *Eraserhead* (1977) all featured characters that tried to survive the decade, as well as the lack of humanity that was rampant in life and film. The independent "mainstream" films of this time also had disturbing insight into the decade, with entries like *Dog Day Afternoon* (1975), *The Deer Hunter* (1978), *Deliverance* (1972) and *Straw Dogs* (1971). If you look at these films while playing disco in the background, you would experience the stark difference between what cinema was reflecting during this time verses that style of music.

It was winter 1977 in Vancouver, B.C. The radio had every song from the movie *Saturday Night Fever* (1977) playing in rotation. I wasn't a disco kid, but the songs had a promise of hope to them. With their shallow pretense, they couldn't have been more mistaken. Their false sense of glitter-filled homes with food and caring people inside was a lie. I was thirteen years old and had just made another escape from the juvenile-scooping task force that would put me through the system of family court, halfway house placements, and bogus foster parents. It was located on Water Street, so we called that arm of the law just that; Water Street.

One night, I found what I thought were three like-minded and similarly aged girls who were staying at their friend's apartment, off the beat, just slightly outside of the city. We all went there to get warm, eat something, and just be safe for a little while. Cindy, the most outspoken and ostensibly the leader of the group, asked me if I wouldn't mind running down to the gas station for some bread so we could make sandwiches. You could see the Shell station from the window. Not far. Maybe a five minute walk, tops. So, being a guest in the runaway sanctuary, I thought it was the least I could do. They gave me a dollar and sent me out for the loaf. I returned to the apartment building and rang the buzzer. Repeatedly. Nothing. So, I yelled up to the apartment from the sidewalk. I saw the girls hanging out the window laughing. I instantly knew I had been taken. I had a loaf of bread in my hands, and they had my purse in theirs. It contained all my worldly possessions: a couple photos, five dollars, a hairbrush, my fake ID, a couple of phone numbers and maybe a few other items, but it was everything I had. They didn't do it for the five bucks; they did it for laughs. They intentionally sent me out to lock me out. I was mad at myself. I had long learned, at this point, not to trust a soul. No one. Ever. I returned the bread to the store and hitchhiked back to the city.

When I got out of the vehicle, I noticed the all-too familiar flashing of lights. It was the cops. After a few questions, and no ID to prove my fake age, eighteen, I found myself in the back of the patrol car. We were headed for Water Street. What happened next would be, what seemed at the time, a most magical thing. The cops got a radio call about an armed robbery and told me to get out. Not questioning this bizarre situation, I was freed. Once they were down the block, I ran. I saw someone I vaguely knew and asked him if he knew a place I could lay low for the night. He took me to an apartment that was occupied by a junkie who bore a resemblance to David Bowie, if you took Bowie, put him in a blender with a Brillo pad and wiped away his good looks. Too skinny, too bleached blond, and too desperate. My acquaintance left the pad and now I was standing in a dumpy apartment whose lease holder's first words to me were "Help me tie off. I'm a wreck." This was the first, and only, time I tried to help a junkie tie off. Try after try after try, his veins just weren't cooperating.

Before he could stick himself to "calm down," there was a knock on the door followed by a deep voice growling about something I couldn't make out. The junkie turns in panic and says "It's my boyfriend, and he's nuts! He knows I scored, but I told him I didn't." The moldy futon I had slept on in the basement at my last foster home came to my mind, and it seemed like a better place right about now. But remembering the abusive adults who ran that fiasco of a "home," I rethought, and I was better off here. At least I could run if things got bad.

The junkie couple started to fight through the apartment's mailbox slot, with the boyfriend slashing a knife through the opening, trying to cut the junkie's face. Then the junkie tried his best to grab the knife, blade side, and his hands were cut and started to bleed. He somehow got the knife from his boyfriend and screamed that he was calling the cops. This seemed to get rid of the guy, but I wondered for how long. I was just looking for a place to lay low for the night, not be witness to multiple felony acts. Now the junkie really needed his junk. He was bleeding pretty fiercely by now, like a lawn sprinkling system. He threw the knife in a drawer then tied off. *Priorities.* He was able to shoot up, then he wrapped his hands in towels to soak up the blood. He became calm, and I became alarmed. I had already seen a lot, but I knew this night was not done. A few people turned up, friends of the junkie, with the guy who brought me there in the first place in tow. I think my concern, which was plastered all over my face, prompted the junkie to give me a valium. I had never taken one before. I was told by everyone at this gathering of low-lifes that it was nothing; it would simply calm me down. I took it, and they all laughed. Within ten minutes, I was passed out cold.

The next thing that I remember were flashes. Quick images of the junkie on top of me humping my leg. I never fully woke up until the next morning. The junkie was gone, and there was no one in the apartment. I still had my underclothes on, but my shirt and jeans were on the floor, blood-stained and cut into pieces. My mind quickly put together the blood was the junkie's from his hand injuries. I puzzled why he had to cut my clothes off. No time for introspection, my goal was to get out of there as quickly as possible, so I rummaged through the room and found a top and pants, threw them on, and fled. Lesson learned. Next time sleep under a bridge or in an underground parking lot. No more handouts.

The series of events I've described happened in one night. So, when you think about surviving three or four years on the street as a juvenile, the volume of life lessons pile-up quick.

While there are beautifully crafted horror movies from every decade, the 1970s hold a special place in my heart for realism, brutality, and the thought that the events you witness while viewing these particular features are, in fact, possible.

It's really no surprise that I have been drawn to underdog and antihero films. Coming out of the time that I did, alive, leaves you with a heightened sense of humanity and, more distinctly, a lack of humanity. What was hard for me was coming back *emotionally* from the 1970s and trying to enter the human race again. Lessons learned are valuable, but you must strive to trust again, at least trust those that deserve it. It has also given me a ton of raw hurt material to draw upon as an actor, and for that I am deeply grateful for my past.

While made in the late 1970s, John Carpenter's *The Thing* was released in 1980. At its core, its sentiment stands as a perfect example of a film testing its character's humanity in a crisis. Not only is it a great horror film, but the movie explores a masterfully crafted through-line of trust and how the characters fold under the pressure of keeping their heads—literally. This horror classic explores the problem of trust in a situation that is designed to destroy any possibility of it existing. But, by the end of the movie, there's a microbe of humanity left in the remaining two characters as they don't simply off one another, though by not doing so they are sure to face their own death. They hold out solely because they still manage a small amount of hope. This is a powerful way to end the story, leaving the true finale in the minds of the audience.

Rod Serling was a master at writing, with the most acute sense of humanity. He was always ahead of his time, and his work was indisputably timeless. He created the most profound television series—*The Twilight Zone*—which aired in the 1960s. It could have aired in any decade and been relevant. He always made a case for or against the possibility of hope. The basis of his writing cut to the bone of what people are made of; how high they might fly if given the chance, or how low they will stoop if given the chance. I saw human behavior that reflected his insights spot-on. Not just in others but with my own highs and lows as a developing teenager. *The Twilight Zone* episode titled "The Monsters Are Due on Maple Street" dealt with mob psychology, a subject that certainly fascinated Serling. This episode shows how quickly a group of people, even if they know each other well, will turn on their neighbors and friends, easily swayed by the words of others. Actor Claude Akins plays the voice of reason, a voice no one wants to hear. Someone who once was a valued member of a community can so easily be rejected and detested because of a mob's uniform way of thinking. Frightening thought. This happens to people every day. This profound ability to plug into human nature is what makes Serling a timeless writer and creator. His work speaks to everyone in any era.

Horror films have an eloquent way of showcasing the underbelly of a prejudiced social class structure. Among the blood, entrails, and decapitations in a great horror movie, there will always be some social reflection or commentary that the writer and director want to say. In my opinion, the films that stand the test of time have both of these elements going on at once; the terror on the surface and the exploration of human nature in the subtext.

Why are these films popular and why do they stand the test of time? Most people have experienced being marginalized, discriminated against, beaten down or simply rejected. We want to see cinematic revenge (*I Spit on Your Grave* [1978]). We want to see vigilantism (*Death Wish* [1974]). We need to see the character who's been beaten in life then have a twist of fate to end up on top somehow. We don't always get what we want, a happy ending of some fashion, even if that means the oppressor gets killed off, but the struggle itself invests us (*The Exorcist* [1973]). The struggle is the thing that keeps us watching.

As artists, it's our personal experiences that make us unique. When you're lucky enough to have the opportunities to creatively use the mounds of excrement you have survived to get to the summit of your personal successes, that's the gold medal. It doesn't always mean everyone will see it or even like your work. But I know when I've had the chance to create something personal that others might relate to, that's my Mount Everest summit. It's not always easy to delve deep. I find my survival mechanisms have a way of blocking access to the scariest, darkest recesses of my memory. It's as though the body itself works overtime to not let certain events surface. Tapping into them can be cathartic. The inner war can be worth it. What comes out the other side will be your truth. And truth will resonate with people.

Looking back, my relationship with disco music was like walking amongst The Ones in Denial, the people who enjoyed the excess of cocaine, anonymous sex, and self-indulgent lifestyles with no guilt. The 1960s started it and the 1970s took it and made it into a Gamera-sized, tinsel monster. That was *my* experience of it. I saw it and analyzed its weakness. Certain men who frequented the boogie bars were depraved enough to pick up very young girls, who either showed their fake ID or their breasts to get into the club. I was there to scope out the worst and drunkest, more than happy to watch them try and pressure me into a sexual encounter. I knew my age, and I had a good idea what their age was. It was repulsive. To a kid looking for a hot meal, they were fair game. Their lack of morals gave me the opportunity and tenacity to slip their wallet off the bar and lighten it of all cash and disappear. Not something to be proud of. Not a quality you would want your child to have. But, if you're going to survive to reach an age that doesn't have 'teen' at the end of it, and you're homeless, you must decide if you want to be victimized or take out a loan from a morally bankrupt sleaze.

Pre-emptive revenge upon the scum was satisfying after everything I had been through. For the first couple of years on my own, I was battered, raped, left for dead; the usual stuff street kids go through. But in reality, I was a punk rock girl. It was punk music that was far more honest and had something to say beyond "You Can Ring My Bell." Punk bands changed the landscape of music. I mean, "Disco Duck?" Oh, hell no, that was for the masses to "get down" to mindlessly on the dance floor. In my world, it was "White Riot" by The Clash that spoke to me, with lyrics like "All the power's in the hands of the rich enough to buy it/while we walk the street too chicken to even try it." By the end of the 1970s, I was a changed person. My "father" was the street and my "mother" was no hope. Unadulterated Charles Dickens material. I am now a completely new and improved person. I live solidly planted in the "pay it forward, find your happiness, be kind to all deserving, and try yoga"—life affirming mantras. Bruce Lee quotes rule my days. I still have flaws. But I'll always have the underdog's back and that will never change.

I will leave the agonizing disco hit "Born to be Alive" to those who enjoy it. I'll be playing "London Calling to the imitation zone/forget it brother, you can go it alone…." Today, you can file me under Lone Wolf, with a heart. My favorite roles to play will always be the "bad guys." I know them well.

The Halloween Family

by Chelsea Stardust

"When ghosts and goblins by the score ring the bell on your front door you better not be stingy or your nightmares will come true!" (Disney's "Trick Or Treat" cartoon, 1952)

TO UNDERSTAND MY LOVE of the horror genre, you first have to understand my love of Halloween. I grew up in the middle of nowhere in Northeast Ohio. Farmlands surrounded my childhood home, with its dusty dirt road, two organic gardens, a sparkling lake, and a white picket fence. It was truly as picturesque as it sounds. My house was only one of three houses on the street with electricity because I grew up in Amish country. Although I was not Amish, we lived in the middle of one of the largest Amish settlements in the world. The rural area meant there was no light pollution, so at night it was pitch black. If there was no moon out you couldn't even see a foot in front of you. You were surrounded with pure darkness.

I'm the daughter (and only child) of two fine artists. My mother is a sculptor, and my father is a painter, both art teachers as well. From a very early age, I was exposed to all kinds of art including some of my favorites like Salvador Dali, Francis Bacon, Man Ray, Anselm Kiefer, Barbara Kruger, Cindy Sherman, and Robert Mapplethorpe. A lot of those artists skew towards the surreal and the provocative. My parents never censored the art I saw, they just tried to nurture my creativity and imagination. I don't even think I knew what censorship was until I was much older.

Both my parents grew up loving Halloween, and they made sure to pass that love on to me. My Amish neighbors didn't celebrate Halloween, so I was never able to trick-or-treat. I could have gone to another neighborhood I guess, but my parents didn't really feel comfortable going somewhere unfamiliar. So they started the tradition of throwing an annual Halloween party. This party was the highlight of the year for me, and because of it, the Halloween season was *everything*.

In August, I would go into our storage closet and pull out all the Halloween decorations. I was *ready* for autumn to arrive and Halloween to grace us with its presence. October was always my favorite month. Once October came, my parents—who always believed having an imagination was one of the most important parts of staying forever young—would start to talk to me as their Halloween alter egos "Mommy Munchkin" (a witchy voice) and "Daddy Dangerous" (something akin to Wolfman Jack). They would chase me through the house as I squealed with terrified delight.

I enjoyed the ritual of preparing for the Halloween party almost as much as the party itself. My mom and I would get out the store-bought decorations and start trimming the house with ceramic jack-o-lanterns, candles shaped like ghosts, black cats, tablecloths and runners featuring autumn colors and foliage, paper skeletons, scarecrow costumes, and more. My dad would check his "Spooky Sounds" vinyl records and make sure they were still scratch-free.

After the house was transformed into a spooky wonderland, we would work on the yard, hand-making a lot of our decorations. Ghosts were created from balled-up newspaper and white trash bags, using Sharpie markers to make eyes and mouths. Mason jars with candles were suspended from trees. Paper lunch bags, with spooky faces carved on the front, were filled with sand and candles and illuminated a path to the front door. Dried cornstalks tied with black and orange ribbon dotted the corners of the house, and a fat scarecrow by the front door, inspired by the short story "Harold" from Alvin Schwartz's *Scary Stories to Tell in the Dark*, greeted our guests. We would rake all the leaves from our big maple trees into a giant leaf pile, and my friends and I would jump and hide inside. We had several black cats, so they added some pretty awesome production value. They all had very fitting names like Morticia, Pyewacket, Mystic Cosmic Creepers Peepers, Magic, Boo, and Shadow.

The Friday before our party was the highlight of the preparations. Our party usually fell on the Saturday before Halloween, and I couldn't wait to get home from school to tackle my favorite part of the decorating process—carving the pumpkins! My dad grew two organic gardens, one entirely dedicated to pumpkins, potatoes, and various squash. He grew huge carving pumpkins and sugar pumpkins for pies. We would harvest five to ten perfect carving pumpkins from the garden, wash them off, and take them inside. I would lay newspaper all over the living room floor and after dinner we would get started. I would clean all the stringy, goopy guts out, and my dad would carve the most incredible designs. A haunted house, a black cat, the Man in the Moon, a ghost! We would watch Cleveland's *Big Chuck & Lil' John's Halloween Special* on WJW Channel 8 and would follow that up with the Universal Monster movies. My personal favorites were always *Dracula* and *The Wolf Man*, but *Frankenstein* and *The Bride of Frankenstein* were loved as well. When I was ten, my dad showed me George A. Romero's *Night Of The Living Dead* which was eventually added into the viewing rotation. I became obsessed with that film, and it's ultimately what pushed me down the path of being a horror film director.

I had nightmares where I accidentally overslept and missed the big Halloween party. Of course that never happened, but the thought *terrified* me. When Saturday came, I would count the hours until the festivities started. I would help my mom prepare all the macabre-themed snacks and drinks (ciders, blood punches, mummy chips & dips), and my dad usually made a pot of chili or my personal favorite—the Midwest classic Sloppy Joes. I was in costume (which I had been planning since April) and ready to rock by 5 p.m. My mom's costumes were always classics. A wicked witch was her favorite, but she also did a regal Egyptian mummy and a rotting plague victim. She was always the "hostess with the mostest." My dad would hide out in the studio while he constructed his costume, arriving casually late to his own party, but his attire always delivered. Sometimes he would show up as a heretic burned at the stake or a road-kill cat. He would also take store-bought masks and transform them into something far more sinister than you'd ever imagine, making it hard for me to even recognize him.

By 8 p.m. the house was filled to the brim with costumed guests, and around 9 p.m. it was time for the Haunted Hayride! The way our property was laid out, we were next door to a Christmas tree farm that had a path leading into the forest that stretched between our home and our neighbors. My parents would coordinate with the neighbors and would have them come down to the party with their tractor and wagon filled with hay bales. We would pile onto the tractor, weaving through the tree farm and into the incredibly spooky forest. They would tell us a scary story about how haunted the woods were, and suddenly we would run into Leatherface, swinging his chainsaw at us! Then a vampire reached out to drag one of us into the night and drink our blood! One after another, characters and creatures would attack our wagon, but we always managed to outrun them. When I was older, my parents spilled the secret and told me they had the neighbor's kids dress up to terrorize us. I was so gullible! But it made the experience all the more fun.

After the hayride, we would run wild in the yard, playing hide-and-seek, tag, and Red Rover. Exhausted, we would eventually head inside and gorge ourselves on hot cider and Munchkins (aka donut holes). Halloween was the *only* time of year I was allowed to have Munchkins, so I savored every single one of them with gleeful delight. When I was older, the "kids' party" was sectioned off to the studio while the adults raged in the house. That is where I exposed my friends to horror film marathons. I would rent as many films as I could get my hands on from the local library, including *Child's Play, Friday the 13th, A Nightmare On Elm Street, Prom Night,* and of course, *Halloween*…all the classic horror fare.

As the witching hour approached, my friends and I would make a big nest on the living room floor with sleeping bags, pillows, and blankets. A lot of folks slept over since we lived so far out in the country and didn't want anyone drinking and driving. I'd fall asleep to the sound of Wilber and Chick trying to escape Dracula and the Monster, the Sanderson Sisters conjuring up another batch of potion, or Scooby-Doo hanging with the Boo Brothers. It was my favorite night of the year, and it was already over as quickly as it had begun.

But the magic of Halloween wasn't done yet. After the party was over and everything was cleaned up, there was still *actual* Halloween to look forward to. It was usually only a few days away too! This was the night when we would watch the Bing Crosby-narrated *The Legend Of Sleepy Hollow,* all the wonderful Walt Disney cartoons ("Trick or Treat," "The Skeleton Dance," "Lonesome Ghosts," "Pluto's Judgement Day," and "Donald & the Gorilla" to name a few) and, last but not least, *It's the Great Pumpkin, Charlie Brown.* Because *Charlie Brown* was one of my favorites, my parents added in an extra splash of magic. They arranged for The Great Pumpkin to visit me every Halloween. I'd write a note to The Great Pumpkin early in the evening, like you'd do for Santa Claus, and right before I went to bed I'd look outside, and there would be a trail of lit jack-o-lanterns leading from our door to the pumpkin patch. I'd follow the trail, almost dying from excitement, and when I arrived at the Pumpkin Patch, there would be candies and spooky gifts for me. I think it was my parents' way of making up for the fact that I couldn't trick-or-treat. They wanted to make sure I had all the Halloween experiences and traditions, even if it meant creating a new one just for me.

This Halloween magic went on for years, pretty much until I moved to California to pursue my dreams as a horror film director. I've been lucky to still hold on to a lot of the traditions my parents instilled in me. I go to a real, authentic pumpkin patch every year and always host a carving party. I watch all of those classic films that I love so much (and the cartoons too), and my parents and I send each other Halloween cards and gifts. Every Halloween night, we talk on the phone and sing the theme from the Donald Duck cartoon "Trick or Treat." I am so thankful I got to have such a magical Halloween experience every year and that I now get to live in a city where there are so many Halloween lovers just like me.

The House That Dripped Dole Whip

by Erin Maxwell

MANY YEARS AGO, my Hebrew studies teacher, a woman with little experience speaking to children other than her own, asked the class a pointed question.

"Ladies, what will you be when you grow up?"

Given that the room was filled with proper Yeshiva girls, the answers were not varied.

"A mother."

"A mother."

"A teacher *and* a mother."

"A vet. And a movie star. Also a singer. And rich."

Wrong answer. As this particular Hebrew seminary didn't even offer math or science for its younger female students, it was safe to say that the school had a specific itinerary in mind for the girls under its instruction.

"Don't be funny. What are you seriously planning?"

I was eight. My long-term plans thus far included eating all the chocolate Rice Krispies before my sister woke up while I watched *Alf Tales*.

"Oh. I'm going to live in the Haunted Mansion."

This event marked the first time I could visibly tell when a grown-up had a headache. It was also possibly the first time Mrs. Seyman questioned the tactic of teaching part-time to get a reduction on tuition for her five children.

Regardless, almost a decade later, this was still my go-to answer when people asked about my possible plans after high school. The only difference is that I traded my tartan pinafore for attire more darkly suitable for my potential digs.

As a teen, I had adopted enough gloomy aesthetics to give my mother pause before she invited friends over. Like many of my cohorts, my dark makeup, black rubber jewelry, and an impressive collection of combat boots certainly gave the impression that I was in need of an ideology. But for the most part, I was fairly typical for a California Cure fan: black hair, black or blood red lipstick, and I loved the Haunted Mansion.

I was like many Southern Californians, dabbling on the edge of the punk and goth scene. I hung out on Melrose, I ate at Okie Dog, and I went to one of the handful of local clubs that catered to the under-eighteen crowds (AntiClub, DDTs, or Helter Skelter). I sported dark hair, dark clothes, dark makeup, and twelve pairs of Doc Martens. I read *Ben is Dead*, Edgar Allen Poe and Neil Gaiman. And I loved Disneyland.

With all my heart.

By the time I was six, I lost count how many times I went to Disneyland. When I was seven, I knew the lay of the land. By eight, I knew all the places Mom would sit and smoke while Dad took us on the fast rides, or the places where Dad could sit and smoke while Mom would take us on indoor rides. Since Disneyland had yet to create a slow moving ride that allowed both children and smoking, there were only a few rides we would all go on together, one of which was the Haunted Mansion. And it was my everything.

As I grew up, my beloved ride grew up with me. It morphed into something a little different, but the overall tone stayed the same. And while the tone was everything, it is important to look back at how the attraction both changed, yet stayed the same, since it opened in 1969.

A short history of the Mansion

In the late 1970s and early 1980s, the ride was slightly different than the version currently running. It wasn't as flashy, lacking both the Hatbox Ghost and Constance Hatchaway, aka the Black Widow Bride, but it was much scarier. While some of my memories are perhaps tinted by youthful exuberance, there were definite changes to the Mansion to calm down the jump scares in an effort to appeal to younger crowds.

Back in the day, the tombstones ghosts lunged at guests with a little more gusto, while Madame Leota's head, though stationary during the seance, insinuated doom and gloom with more zeal. The screams for help from behind the doors and crypts were accompanied by hidden frights and loud shrieks which have since been muffled.

According to Haunted Mansion history, it appears that prior to my childhood visits, the Mansion was even more terrifying. Even alarming.

Once upon a time, there was a real person as the Knight in Armour, a character located in the beginning of the ride where the Endless Hallway now stands. Unfortunately, due to the efficiency of scaring the bejesus out of guests, the Knight was retired after a short tenure. Now, much like the tales of the cremated dead mixed with the faux dust of the manor, it is all part of urban legend.

The Mansion is located in New Orleans Square, right between Frontierland and Adventureland, two lands that fit within Walt Disney's idealism, as they represent a fantasy walkabout of the studio's live action library. Within the Square sits Pirates of the Caribbean, a smart move for Disney, who at the time of construction, was releasing the occasional pirate movie such as *Treasure Island (1950)*, their first foray into live-action feature entertainment. It is important to note that this was before Johnny Depp donned a first-rate Keith Richards impersonation; back in the day when the pirates chased the women, not the other way around. The randy pirates were changed over the years due to both growing sensitivities and because "The Sexual Assault-iest Place on Earth" was a hard sell on a t-shirt...even in rhinestones. Regardless, Pirates of the Caribbean made perfect sense insofar as a thematic statement of the ride.

Initially, the idea of the Haunted Mansion came about in the late '50s as a walk-through attraction with a sea-theme that would keep with the story of Pirates of the Caribbean. In fact, early versions of the ride connected the two attractions with a pirate storyline. Original interpretations of the Mansion centered on a story of a sea captain named Capt. Bartholomew Gore, a man with a secret who marries an innocent young bride. When she discovers he is actually an evil pirate, he kills the young lady. He is then haunted by her ghost until he takes his own life, an act that beckons more ghosts and ghouls to join them in their eternal afterlife.

Hey kids, welcome to the happiest place on Earth!

"King of Animation" Marc Davis helped give shape to the inhabitants of the Mansion, as he had to nearby Pirates, Jungle Cruise natives, and the singing squawkers of the Enchanted Tiki Room. Early renditions of the Mansion also included magic tricks and illusions, as well as a Museum of the Weird that would showcase odd creatures and sideshow acts. The brainchild of Imagineer Rolly Crump, the high-concept attraction focused more on the surreal than scary.

As for the exterior, original sketches of the would-be Haunted Mansion depicted the attraction as a run-down residence, similar to the digs in Robert Wise's 1963 adaptation of the Shirley Jackson classic story *The Haunting of Hill House*. It was also to be located off Main Street rather than across the way from Tom Sawyer's Island. Eventually, these nightmarish notions were discarded as Walt's interest waned through the early '60s. It wasn't until Mr. Disney's passing that enthusiasm in the spooky estate was sparked again.

Inspired by the Shipley-Lydecker House in Baltimore, construction on the antebellum-style manse began to move forward in the late 1960s, sans the themes of murderous sea captains or the Museum of the Weird, although evidence of both those concepts are still present in the Mansion today. The iconic eye-pattern wallpaper in the hallway is reminiscent of Crump's early designs while the ship-shaped weather vane on the top on the Mansion stands as a monument to early versions of the twisted tale.

When the Mansion opened in 1969, guests were left with a jaw-dropping experience that only Disney could deliver. While the story was slightly disjointed, it nonetheless did the job and delivered thrills, chills and scares galore to unsuspecting crowds. The Haunted Mansion was a success.

There we have a quick history of the Mansion, but still, it doesn't explain why it is in Disneyland. Aside from the occasional Don Knotts movie, there is not a lot in the Disney catalog that suggests scary. Traumatizing, sure. But not intentionally scary. Even with the removal of the bloodthirsty Captain Gore, the Haunted Mansion is downright morbid.

For many reasons, the Haunted Mansion is out of place, the first of which is the dark, macabre nature of the ride. The cemeteries, the fiends, the unholy terrors that creep and crawl. And while the ride picks up in the second half to good-natured goofy (not Goofy) fun with ghosts and ghouls, there is something far more sinister about the ten-minute excursion. After all, you don't see Nanna the St. Bernard or the Mad Hatter urging guests to off themselves in the first few minutes of their dark-ride outings, do you?

Themes of suicide, murder and the unsettling nature of this particular notion of the afterlife are decidedly not Disney. And while it can be explained with forgotten backstories and half-hearted attempts to create a connective tissue between the nearby attractions, the dark concept of the ride is still somewhat unsettling if you linger. Indeed, the Haunted Mansion sticks out like a sore thumb amidst the pixie dust.

It is the ghoulish charm of the Mansion that attracts the fringe to the most family-friendly place on planet Earth. Yes, the Mansion doesn't fit in with the look and feel of Disney. Nothing about it is adorable or quaint.

It is the odd duck of Disneyland, which is why weirdos are attracted to it. The darkness of it all, mixed with urban legends and the macabre history act as a beacon for those on the periphery of normal. The Haunted Mansion stands as a symbol to those who partake in counterculture.

Being goth in California is like being a Haunted Mansion in Disneyland. It might not fit into the sunny environment, but made itself at home in an unlikely habitat all the same. Just as the Haunted Mansion is seemingly out of place in the Happiest Place on Earth, it draws like-minded individuals who feel the same about themselves: those who don't mesh with the vibe of Walt's vision, but still love thrill rides, frosted Dole Whip treats, and balloons could find themselves peace of mind within the damask walls no matter their age.

For the most part, Southern California goths love Disneyland. Unabashedly, whole heartedly, and without sarcasm or cynicism. The wholesome look of Main Street and the upbeat, fuzzy characters who inhabit the park do little to deter the somber adolescent masses who often flock to the gates for year-round fun. It is perhaps one of the more bizarre traits amongst the SoCal goth scene: to love the darkness while holding the same unabashed love for the Happiest Place on Earth. While those who dabble in dark subcultures from other regions tend to turn their nose up at the mere idea of visiting anything as family-friendly as Disneyland, SoCal goths (and many who moved to the area) have a different modus operandi.

It's simple to understand why. Behind the sunny guise, there is a dark heart to the park. Dark, dingy, filled with dead things, the Doombuggies are chariots waiting to take melancholy fans away on a ten-minute tour of the spirit realm. Growing up within a close proximity to Disneyland has an effect on many SoCal kids. Visiting Disneyland isn't just an event that occurs every few years and is remembered in pictures, but an annual event… or more. For some, Disneyland is a playground visited many, many times during the course of the year.

For us SoCal kiddies, it was our first exposure to anything dark or sinister. Mom and Dad controlled the family car radio, movies, and television, so introductions to subcultures were not easily accessible to the Cabbage Patch crowd. The Haunted Mansion opened a squeaky door to an eerie netherworld that wasn't dominated by cheerful cartoon characters. It was something exciting and scary and altogether new for gangs of young children who might not have a way to express their feelings, which might not have always been chipper.

As these kids grew and their tastes developed, those who felt at home in the shadows often cited the Haunted Mansion as their first foray into the macabre. It was the monster starter kit that set young'uns on the track towards horror movies and Bauhaus. It was a statement that proudly said, "Scary but fun," which became the mantra of many a twisted teen.

As a teenager, Disneyland was home away from home for me. I romped through the park with the same gusto I had in my childhood. And still I believed the Mansion was the perfect residence. It offered a large attic and a ballroom with decor that matched my taste.

After my teen years, after my parents sold our duplex, it was hard to find a place that felt like my childhood digs. In the years after college, I moved ten times in ten years. With each move, I felt less and less settled. But the Haunted Mansion was always there for me. Standing as it always did, it was a special place where my childhood memories resided. I could always return (for a price), the way college students and young adults come home for the holidays. And I wasn't alone in my worship.

In 1999, all those who fell under the sway of the Haunted Mansion decided to make a day of it, as Bats Day in the Park was first established. Once called the "largest dark subculture on the West Coast," the fine folks of Bats Day celebrated those who worshiped the eerie with a two-day gathering in Anaheim. Not a costumed event, but a gathering of Gothabillies, Rivetheads, Steampunks, and more who enjoy a ride on a flying elephant as much as the next dark soul. The annual event was always held in August during the dog days of summer, a bad time for those who enjoy black clothes and white makeup, but a good time to still make use of summer vacation while avoiding blackout dates on the Disney annual pass. And for that weekend, Disneyland was a spectacle to behold as Deathrockers would laugh their way through rocket rides while Baby Bats made their way to the submarines.

It was the Haunted Mansion that was the centerpiece of the event, as hundreds would flock to its iron gates during the Bats Days. Setting up faux picnics on the lawn, staging wedding photos and bringing flowers to the dearly departed four-legged friends who reside forever in the line queue, the participants of Bats Day paid homage to their temple with the proper respect and decorum. Alas, all good things must end. In 2018, an announcement was made that while the park meet-up would still occur, the official Bats Day in the Park full weekend was no more.

In the past, the Haunted Mansion influenced thousands, inadvertently introducing young guests to a penumbra of gloom that would shape their lives. Now in the modern era, the Haunted Mansion not only continues to weave its spell over new generations, but over those who shape culture as well. Filmmakers, scribes and songwriters alike pull from the Haunted Mansion for influence in their craft as the Mansion became an icon of the horror genre.

The Haunted Mansion has gone through many changes and renovations through the years. It went from spooky with a disconnected story to high tech with less jump scares. Skeletal brides with beating red hearts doomed to forever listen to the wedding march, have been replaced with serial killers who gleefully show off an abundance of dead husbands. The hall of portraits has been home to many a different visage, moving from the slowly morphing image to the lightning crash quick scare. In recent years, the legendary Hatbox Ghost, the iconic phantom whose brief debut in the Mansion was riddled with technical difficulties, finally found his rightful place in the monster manor.

And of course, each Halloween to Christmas, the Haunted Mansion puts on a costume, smells of gingerbread, and attempts to sell you a Hot Topic hoodie when *The Nightmare Before Christmas* (1993) takes over the Mansion. But as much as everything changes, things still remain the same. The entrance still smells of musk as a somber pipe organ welcomes you to board an elevator. The lifeless eyes of the concave busts still follow your every move as you wander down the hall. The metal monsters on the top of each stanchion still sit, their facial features rubbed down to nubs due to the thousands of grimy hands that have touched them over the years. The Doombuggies still await to take you away. In turn, you walk a little faster, fueled by the fear of missing a moving target and falling in front of other guests.

As you go down the hall, you find that the ghosts are still attempting to break into the hallway where the same four or five ghoulish portraits hang on the walls and the clock goes to thirteen. Madame Leota is still working her charms and the ballroom is as lively as ever. Gus, Ezra and Phineas still hope to hitch a ride home with you at the end of your excursion. And the bullet hole in the large pane of glass in the ballroom scene, created long ago by a misfired BB gun, is still hidden with a well-placed spider. All of the elements so keenly etched into childhood are there. Small changes are fine. Even Walt Disney himself, who was more pragmatic than nostalgic, probably would have approved.

At the end of the day, the Haunted Mansion, and most of Disneyland, is a small part of many people's childhood. And unlike life, it rarely changes. It remains in New Orleans Square just beyond the iron gates and the ghost horse-drawn hearse. And while other parts of Disneyland have the same appeal, few have had the same impact on spirit or personality as the Haunted Mansion.

As an adult, one can find themselves lost. Perhaps parents have passed away or childhood homes were sold long ago. Time has a way of fracturing families and friendships. Finding those key pieces of the past become harder and harder to track down. Understanding key elements of a person's growth might only be a distant memory told over shared bottles of wine. Visiting such places is harder as time marches on. But that is not the case with the Mansion.

For many, the Haunted Mansion is a novelty haunted house, with a bigger budget than those found at fun fairs; a grown-up version of the old Pretzel Rides from the two-bit carnivals of yore. But for me, and many like me, it is more than that. It is a touchstone. It is what made me curious about monster movies and turned me into a horror hound. It is responsible for my black and purple wardrobe. It is why I wear black eyeliner. The Haunted Mansion started me on a path that helped me define who I am. And because it stands in New Orleans Square, I can visit it anytime. The Haunted Mansion is more than an attraction. It is a benchmark of my being. It is where I return time and time again to reclaim my childhood and the memories of family and friends.

It is home.

The Ghosts of Berg's Video

by Rhianne Paz Bergado

IN ORDER TO UNDERSTAND my love affair with horror movies, you have to see the whole picture. My story doesn't even begin with myself; it starts a whole ocean away with the deviant, school-ditching boy named Raul who would grow up to be my father. My dad grew up in the Philippines with my grandfather who was a handyman and mechanic for Fernando Poe Sr., an actor-turned-director in the Filipino movie industry; the Philippines' own Clark Gable. Bearing in mind that this was wartime of the 1940s, it's worth mentioning that Raul himself entered this world with a bang. During the bombings in the Philippines of World War II, my grandmother suddenly threw him out a window fearing that their home was going to collapse. I'm convinced that this little stunt is proof that my father was destined to become an action film junkie.

After World War II, my dad, like many young Filipinos, was obsessed with American war movies, musicals, and Westerns of the time. He would go to the movie theater where his uncle was the security guard. They had a system where they would signal the ticket taker and when the coast was clear, my dad would scurry into the theater and watch whatever movie he wanted. He was a film-addict, just like his daughter was to become.

There are a lot of old-timey ghost stories from the Philippines that I feel added to the DNA of my family and ultimately ended up molding me into a horror fan and filmmaker. It doesn't hurt that culturally, ghost stories and legends run rampant in the culture. We believe in the "White Lady," a woman in a nightgown who haunts Balete Drive in Quezon City; the "Aswang," a disemboweled spirit that steals babies from wombs with her tongue; and an assortment of headless nuns and priests for good measure. There's even a movie that includes my family name, *Bergado: The Terror of Cavite*. While it's still unknown if my family is tied to this film in any way, I remain delighted just to have my name on an action-packed 1970s exploitation film.

After the war, my father's family moved in with Fernando Poe Sr.'s family. The late 1930s through the wartime of the forties was the golden era of cinema not only in America but in the Philippines as well, so the family home was a mansion, complete with swimming pool. One day, as a child, my father fell into the pool. Not knowing how to swim, he began to sink but he suddenly felt a tug at his shirt and was lifted to the surface. As he came to, there was not a soul in sight; he was completely alone in the pool. The universe had bigger plans for little Raul.

In the 1970s, my father got the chance to immigrate to America with my mother and, even though he had a degree as a mathematician and my mom was qualified to teach, they were seen as foreigners and ended up as laborers in makeup factories and fish canneries. The 1980s saw the boom of the VCR in America's homes and as my parents rose in ranks and income, my family was eventually able to open a VHS rental business called "Berg's Video."

Now, let's pause and reflect on the romance and magic that was the local, mom and pop video store of the 1980s. We currently have endless amounts of films and shows streaming straight into our home televisions and even into our pockets, but back then, you had to go to a strip mall video store to rent a movie. It was a magical place filled with posters and shelves that smelled like plastic and cardboard. There were brightly colored neon stickers that labeled each VHS tape as Comedy, Drama, or Horror. You would have to talk to a clerk about new releases. You would physically hold the box in your hand and read the movie synopsis on the back.

As you can imagine, growing up in a video store was not a common thing for most kids. I was exposed to a constant stream of movies and, to a greater extent, artwork that shaped my tiny, impressionable mind into what it is today. Most movies had "presentable" artwork, but it was the horror and fantasy movies that stuck with me the most. The 1980s were a time before Photoshop and if you wanted to generate epic imagery, studios had to rely on actual painters and illustrators that worked with their hands to deliver the goods. We had artists like Renato Casaro painting movie posters for *Conan the Barbarian* (1982) and James Bond. Drew Struzan was known for his legendary work on *Star Wars*, *Indiana Jones*, and *Blade Runner* (1982). I have distinct memories of the first time I saw images for movies like *House* (1985), a simple disembodied zombie hand ringing a doorbell, or the image of a wolf's mouth extending out of a human mouth on the poster for *The Company of Wolves* (1984). I have a soft spot for the movie *April Fool's Day* (1986), solely based on the cover image of a girl offering a toast with a knife behind her back and her hair braided into a noose. It was a great era for the horror movie.

Every week, studios would send us promotional items for movies, and no one loves useless, promotional items more than an immigrant Filipino family. Somehow, we convinced ourselves that all these free, plastic tchotchkes were the perfect accent to the sophisticated decor of our home, which consisted of fiber optic light-up plants and a giant wooden spoon and fork hanging on the wall. My sister and I would plaster movie posters edge-to-edge all over our walls and even on the ceiling of our bedroom, making a solid box of movie memorabilia. We had a *Teen Wolf* (1985) mug that would turn the character into a wolf when you'd fill it with hot water and, of course, we had a cardboard cutout of Freddy Krueger himself which would terrify me nightly when we had to turn off the lights and lock up the store.

My routine for the day included coming "home" from school to the storage room of the video store. I would stop at the liquor store two doors down, load up on SweeTarts and Twix bars, and start my shift. We had a couch of questionable smells and origins, a small TV and VCR, and an army of video rewinding machines, which was my specialty as a six-year-old. We also had a microfiche machine to view catalogs of the films we could order. You may know these machines best from movies where detectives look at old newspaper articles to research a small town's murder history. I usually used it like a carnival ride where I would spin the images on the screen around and around until it made me dizzy and I fell off the office chair. It was a fun time to be a kid. I had a buffet of all the movies I could watch, and all the artwork I could consume.

To understand why horror movies proliferated in the 1980s, we have to look at what took place in the tumultuous 1970s. Our definition of fear changed because the things we feared in real life had evolved. We had experienced our first televised war on color television. Our news was no longer shot and edited by the US government and packaged for us a month later as it was during WWII; it was "Live and in Color!" We developed distrust for the government and grew a bit more cynical as a country. By the 1980s, Halloween had graduated from being a cute kid's holiday to a holiday celebrated by adults. There was a real sense of fear after rumors of poisoned candy and Halloween kidnappings became sensationalized on the nightly news. We got into the habit of fear, so it was only natural that our art and media reflected it. Even children's movies were dark: *Return to Oz* (1985), *Watcher in the Woods* (1980), *The Dark Crystal* (1982), *Labyrinth* (1986), and *Legend* (1985) were definitive signs of the times.

Horror movies were a low-budget solution to a world that was experiencing home video for the first time. We were creating new symbols of pop culture, our own Draculas and Frankenstein's monsters. Not until the late 1970s or early 1980s were we allowed to imagine a new generation of "boogeymen" to seep into the mainstream. Michael Meyers, Jason Voorhees, and Freddy Krueger became household names and the era of the horror franchise was born.

By the late 1980s, home video was big business but my family knew it was the beginning of the end when The Wherehouse started a video rental section. They had a huge selection of movies, a staff of five to six employees working at all times, and, most importantly, they had five to ten copies of popular movies, which was hard to compete with considering that a VHS movie could run $50 to $90 a copy. It was tough to compete, and luckily we had sold the store before Blockbuster came into the market to obliterate us. Along with closing the store, we moved to a new town, but everything I absorbed in that little storage room stayed with me. As a teenager, I had a macabre fascination with comics, sci-fi, horror, and exploitation movies. By the time I graduated from high school, I was toting a portfolio to Comic-Con and had my eyes set on animation school. I ended up studying both film and animation in college.

Like most production people, I had an unpredictable and wandering path into the world of filmmaking. I went from local news to reality TV, to making content for Disney, and ended up at a little television network called FEARnet. Like most alumni of this tight-knit family, I still regard my five years working directly in the horror industry as one of the greatest adventures of my life. I felt like I had come full circle, and I could see the tiny, six-year-old Mowgli version of me swell with pride at where I had landed. Every week I was sitting in a room with a legend or icon of my youth. I was able to hear Jamie Lee Curtis talk about *Halloween* (1978) two feet away from me; I shook hands with Sir Anthony Hopkins; I stood on the trapdoor where Margaret Hamilton played the Wicked Witch; I shot a private interview with Mark Hamill; and even directed John Kassir, the voice of the Crypt Keeper himself. (To be clear, there is no such thing as "directing" John Kassir; you just kind of sit there with your mouth open in awe as the magic flows out of him.) The most notable experience that tied together my video store youth with my adult career came when we spent a week in a small town in Ohio. We were shooting behind-the-scenes footage for *Fear Clinic* (2009). Playing the Fear Doctor himself was Robert Englund, or as I knew him, the Freddy Krueger cardboard cutout that terrorized my youth. Spending time on set, I learned that Robert was one of the smartest people I was ever going to meet. He could talk at length about just about any subject, from quantum physics to the history of carnival posters; his knowledge was far and wide. But here I was, a tiny brown daughter of an immigrant having a conversation with Freddy Krueger on a snowy Ohio day.

Working in the horror industry is like a boot camp for indie film. You learn to work hard, work fast, work cheap, and you discover why the industry is such a small community. The horror industry has a unique brand of geek that's willing to take a single amazing scene and argue that it makes up for what would otherwise be a terrible film.

I think that most people are surprised that the horror audience is pretty much split down the middle in terms of male and female fans and is actually quite diverse. While we hardly see Black and Latinx stories in mainstream cinema, the presence and desires of these audiences have existed for a long time. Fear and horror are a universal language; just about anyone can identify with a good scary movie. The best part of horror narratives is that the stakes are always incredibly high. In a drama or romantic comedy, we worry about whether the boy will get the girl or if the family will stay together but in a horror movie, it's always life or death. The trope of "the Final Girl" is also an incredibly old depiction of the fact that women can and will find a way to survive, no matter how uneven the playing field may seem. The horror movie, in its own way, has been a feminist symbol far before we made a Pinterest board about it.

These days, I make a living producing and directing content in the beauty and fashion space. The production family I built at FEARnet is still with me, and we've all grown into amazing cinematographers, editors, and production designers in our own right. Once a year, we're able to flex our old FEARnet skills when we get to make a commercial Halloween video. We like to reminisce and talk about the "old days" (just five or six years ago) when we lived and breathed Halloween 24/7, 365 days a year. Working in that small team was like being a scrappy film student all over again. We worked hard and exerted our talents with limited resources and tons of heart. That scrappy fighting spirit brings me back to the days of growing up in a strip mall. We passed out flyers advertising my parents store on foot, and used a kitchen utensil organizer as a cash box because we couldn't afford a cash register. Raul is retired now, and when I asked him about how he felt about the video store thirty years later, he simply said: "I liked those days, we were happy."

I love horror movies because they remind me of what it's like to be afraid of what's coming next. They allow us to confront our fears about death and the ghosts of our past from the comfort of our couches. At the end of the day, perhaps it's just fun to make light of our fragile humanity. It's healthy to exercise our ability to make art and tell stories about our demons. Maybe horror fans are more in touch with our humanity than the world thinks we are.

The Bisexual Energy of *I Know What You Did Last Summer* Was a Peak 1990s Sexual Awakening

by Haleigh Foutch

I KNOW WHAT YOU DID LAST SUMMER (1997) is not the best 1990s teen horror movie, but it is the thirstiest. Take a second to think of the most iconic imagery in the history of slasher cinema: Michael's mask. Freddy's glove. Leatherface's chainsaw. Even Ghostface, if we want to stick with the 1990s. The iconic moments in slashers are killer-oriented; it's why slasher franchises can endure endless sequels, reboots, and reimagining. It's all about the killer.

But *I Know What You Did Last Summer* is a different kind of slasher—a true blue 1990s teen drama lightly draped in the trappings of teen slasherdom. Sure, there's murder and revenge and more murder, but above all, *I Know What You Did Last Summer* is a young adult narrative about the drama that unfolds between a tight-knight group of friends. Hell, the killer is introduced as an afterthought literally moments before he's revealed, which is why it's not the sight of the hook or the fisherman's coat that endures in *I Know What You Did Last Summer*'s legacy. Nope, this movie was made for thirsty teens, which means it's Ryan Phillipe's glistening abs, Sarah Michelle Gellar's flowing hair, and Jennifer Love Hewitt's "ample" breasts, barely concealed in a semi-see-through tank top as she screams "What are you waiting for?!" into the sky.

Those fleshy fascinations were the talk of the town among me and my girlfriends in 1997, giggling tweens staring wide-eyed at our favorite celebrities, shirtless and crop-topped, toned for the gods and costumed (or not costumed) to summon the full force of teenage lust. And boy, did it. *I Know What You Did Last Summer* was a sexual revelation in my circles, a constant topic of discussion and obsession in gym class, at lunch, and during those endless after-school phone calls where you debated if you were more of a Ryan Phillippe or Freddie Prinze Jr. girl (Phillippe, obviously. Two years later it would be Prinze), Type O Negative's "Summer Breeze" cover blaring in the background.

It wouldn't be right to say that *I Know What You Did Last Summer* isn't interested in the male gaze in horror (and the script certainly does no favors in the chauvinism department), but at least it was a valiant champion of equal objectification. Yes, Hewitt's boobs were not at all subtly the emphasis of a lot of screen time, but so was Phillipe's towel-draped torso and the brigade of pre-superhero era biceps, flaunted in tighter v-necks and tank tops than should be legal in a teen drama.

Meanwhile, Sarah Michelle Gellar's beauty queen Helen Shivers never stops serving peak late-1990s lewks; working cutoff shorts, metallic armbands, and headbands as thick as her extensions. It didn't hurt that Gellar was a true teen queen and a personal hero for me, a *Buffy the Vampire Slayer* diehard who thought Gellar was the be-all, end-all of all things cool. *I Know What You Did Last Summer* arrived in theaters in the thick of Buffy's second season, and Gellar was a bona fide superhero in my eyes—the ass-kicking, fast-quipping fashion icon I aspired to be. Helen Shivers was no Buffy Summers, but she was the best film role Gellar ever landed, and damn, she was fierce.

Like many teen girls, the relationship I had with the bodies and beauty of the celebrities I admired was complicated and often confused. Sarah Michelle Gellar's petite frame made me feel great strength when she fought off the big bads in *Buffy the Vampire Slayer*—if she could do it, so could I—but it also gave me that teenage body confidence crisis; setting a standard that would never be possible with my body type. I strived for Gellar's willowy frame, for the way spaghetti strap shirts fell on her slight shoulders like they were crowning her the queen of 1990s fashion. More than once, I wrapped my entire torso in duct tape to make my dresses fit more like hers. But I didn't just want to be like her. In a strange conflict no doubt familiar to many bisexual women, I didn't just wish I could be her; I wished I could be *with* her—the lines between admiration, competition, and attraction all mixed up in tension and anxiety I hadn't yet learned to untangle.

And swoon, there were the heartthrobs—Phillippe and Prinze were the crème de la crème of *Teen Beat* sweethearts in 1997; a pair of heartbreaking hotties who kept the margins of my notebook full with heart-encased doodles. Between the two of them, Gellar and Hewitt, the film was a veritable buffet of babes, and it was somewhere between Phillipe's heart-stopping locker room scene (and I don't mean because it's scary) and Jennifer Love Hewitt's increasingly exposed midriff that I started to realize I might just be attracted to everyone in the movie.

It's not just me. The bisexual energy in *I Know What You Did Last Summer* is so strong it should come with a youth counselor for confused teens. The star power of the teen heartthrobs is powerful enough, but then there's the fact that the film accidentally makes a stronger case for Helen and Julie (Hewitt) as a couple than providing a convincing reason for either of the enchanting ladies to be shunted off with their frankly horrid romantic leads. On top of being an alcoholic and a walking dick, Barry (Phillippe) is an abusive mess, and gormless, guppy-mouthed Ray (Prinze) is just as bad; the well-actually "good guy" who would definitely be the killer in a modern update.

But Julie and Helen are both smart and ambitious, and together, they have Capital-C Chemistry. Combine that with a dash of (almost certainly unintentional) queer-baiting ambiguity in the script, and magnetism in their performances, and you've got the start of a real adolescent fascination. If *I Know What You Did Last Summer* came out now, I have no doubt there would be "Jelen" or "Hulie" shipping blogs all over Tumblr. When Helen confronts Julie in her car midway through the film, she asks "What happened to us? We used to be friends." Julie snaps back with, "We used to be a lot of things," and rationally, we know she's talking about when they weren't, you know, murderers, but the delicious ambiguity of it leaves just a wide enough crack in the door for the mind to wander through.

All things considered, watching *I Know What You Did Last Summer* for the first time was an intense experience in self-awakening for this hormonal little pre-teen. So naturally, I watched it with my father, a self-professed scaredy cat, who jumped so high at an especially cheap jump scare that he nearly sent us both flying onto the floor. If there's one thing that can put a magnifying glass on a moment of sexual awakening, it's the profoundly awkward experience of having one in the presence of your own terrified parent. But I'm glad I have that memory. In fact, it's one I cherish. I never got to come out to my dad—he died the same year we watched the film together, long before I fully understood and owned my own sexuality, or before I was in a position to be coming out to anybody. But the fact that he was part of my coming out narrative, that he was a part of a formative experience that helped me know myself better, even in the most casual, unintentional way, has always given me a measure of comfort.

I'm not saying that *I Know What You Did Last Summer* made me realize I'm queer—that was a long process that started with an unusually intense need to impress this one girl at summer camp and ended with a silly internet quiz telling me what I already knew: "You're Bisexual." But *I Know What You Did Last Summer* was an important stepping stone on the path to self-acceptance and understanding; like one of the lenses that snaps into place at the optometrist and helps you see the full picture: you're not quite there, the edges are still blurry, but that lens helped make everything just a bit clearer.

Horror Lifestyle

David Cronenberg's Guide To Childbirth: Reflections On Being a Horror-Loving Parent

by Rebekah McKendry

FOR THE BULK OF MY "ADULT" LIFE, I did not want kids. I did not really like children of any age but was especially irritated by younger ones with runny noses and a penchant for repeatedly asking "why." I know it is weird to have this feeling considering that at one point I was a high school teacher, but I quickly realized I didn't want to be a high school teacher either. After a hellish semester spent as a student teacher for various elementary school grade levels, I found children to be mildly amusing, but generally repugnant in extended doses.

I had seen the horror of a six-year-old getting a wild, unstoppable nosebleed all over my classroom desks, books, and floor. I simultaneously tried to comfort the kid and rush them to the clinic all while suiting up in latex gloves that went up to my elbows and trying to recall where I had stashed the industrial strength classroom bleach. It was at this moment that I decided kids were probably not my ideal career or life choice. I followed my dreams and pursued a career working in the horror industry and also adopted a dog. Then two dogs. I became a very happy dog owner and Fangoria employee.

Even while all our friends began procreating, my husband Dave and I stuck to our unfruitful ways. We sat quietly during conversations of diaper sales and the best day care, all the while secretly relishing our super clean house and disposable income. And for a decade nothing changed.

They all had little nosepickers; I had the ability to leave the house anytime I wanted, go to midnight horror movie screenings, and sleep until noon on weekends.

Then it happened. At age thirty-six, I woke up one morning with the sudden urge to procreate. What the fuck? Must be the flu. But there it was the next day. And the next. And the next. I sheepishly mentioned it to my husband and discovered he too was feeling this peculiar urge for... a baby.

Why? Where had this come from? Were we ready for that? Well, not at all to be honest. We had just impulsively moved to Los Angeles to pursue our love of the horror genre, I was working full-time for Fangoria but still living paycheck to paycheck, often making decisions about whether I should get that painful tooth fixed or have food for the next week, and we shared an apartment with other people. But we figured what the hell—let's give it a try, and we will have at least nine months to figure something out.

I found out I was pregnant at San Diego Comic Con. We arrived at the mothership of all geek exhibitions on Tuesday morning and started setting up the Fangoria booth which I was in charge of for the week. This was all standard as we had attended SDCC for five years prior, and I knew exactly what to expect. It was hectic, stressful, and so claustrophobic you wanted to drop kick every person dressed as Deadpool by the third day, but it was nothing I couldn't handle.

Thursday morning, I woke up and proceeded to vomit for a solid fifteen minutes in the bathroom of room #401 at the San Diego Comfort Inn Suites. I then cleaned myself up and slowly walked down to the lobby bathroom where my body continued to evacuate everything I had eaten for about two weeks prior. Could this be it? Is this awful gut-wrenching purging an indication that I'm pregnant? Is me curled over a toilet in a hotel restroom heaving with every muscle in my body the start of the magic of pregnancy or just a sign the sushi I ate last night may have been less fresh than the flashing neon buffet sign indicated?

I somehow managed to stop the dry heaving and compose myself enough to walk to a CVS. I bought a pregnancy test and ginger ale, and then headed to the convention hall. We were supposed to have a big staff meeting at 9 a.m. before the convention floor opened. There were already thousands of attendees lining up outside, and I elbowed my way through and stood in line to use the bathroom. Yes, you *always* have to stand in line to use the bathroom at San Diego Comic Con. *Always*. Nestled in between a group of Tomb Raider cosplayers and the human version of a *My Little Pony*'s Rainbow Dash, I contemplated the test I was about to take.

Should I do it now in the public bathroom of the San Diego convention center, surrounded by giggling pop culture fiends?

Shouldn't I do this in a slightly classier environment or someplace with meaning?

You know what—this has meaning for me. And if I'm going to find out that I'm in the process of making some type of human spawn, I realized it should, of all places on earth, be here. If I'm going to pee on a stick and stare at it for five minutes to learn my entire fate, I want to examine that urine-soaked stick in these surroundings. I love pop culture! I love fandom! I loved the Rainbow Dash human/pony hybrid in front of me and was also quite curious how she was going to get out of the elaborate pony costume to use the bathroom. But finally, it was my turn. A sexy Pikachu emerged from the third stall of the left, and it was my turn. This was it.

Waiting waiting waiting. All I could think of was *The Simpsons* episode where Apu and his wife take the pregnancy test, and the "positive" emblem was a pirate. Come on pirate! Come on pirate! Two lines appeared. Wait. There are two lines. Holy fuck. I'm pregnant… I'm pregnant?… I'm pregnant!!! Wait… I'm pregnant…. What the fuck now?!?

I had to tell Dave! I then realized Dave was likely sitting at the Fangoria booth with all the rest of my staff waiting for me to come strolling in and start the morning staff meeting. I knew there was no way I was going to be able to just causally walk in and start talking about the importance of how we fold the Fangoria t-shirts and stack them by size. So…. I'll text him. Yes, so he'll know, and I won't have to announce it in front of my whole staff. So I snapped a picture of the test with the lovely San Diego Convention Center latrine in the background. I flushed first, cause…. ya know, I wanted it to be a classy picture. Dave met me on the convention floor smiling and gave me a huge hug. Holy Fuck. We were gonna be parents. My brain began racing with every pregnancy horror film I had ever seen… *Rosemary's Baby* (1968), *Baby Blood* (1990), *Grace* (2009), *Xtro* (1982). Yikes, no not *Xtro*, let's just not think about that one.

I have heard so many women talk about how beautiful pregnancy is. I read books where people referred to it as a magical and spiritual time. Even my best friend sat me down to tell me about how the next nine months of my life would be a miraculous discovery of just how amazing and transcendent the female body can be. Bullshit. All of it…. Total damn bullshit.

Though I was excited as hell about having a baby, I hated pregnancy. Seriously hated it. My back hurt, my feet swelled, and I had insane heart burn. I also developed a strange hunger for meat in all forms. Usually, I follow a fairly vegetarian diet with occasional sinful days of sushi. But while pregnant I would have eaten the face off a cow if I could have waddled close enough to one. I also slathered everything with Tabasco (seeing now why the heartburn was such a thing). I ate jalapenos straight out of the jar…sometimes with lunchmeat wrapped around them. I was experiencing the plot line of a horror film. I hadn't seen this specific one, but instead was living it. I hungered for meat, all the while my body was out of control. I was going through a Cronenbergian transformation, and all I could do was sit back, watch it happen, and eat a burger.

I grew bigger and bigger. I binge watched endless horror films, distracting myself from the fact that something was coming. Something big. One night as I sat on my couch binging giallo titles, my stomach moved. I looked down. My entire abdomen shuddered and wiggled. I touched it. It jumped in a different direction. Then an unknown appendage pushed out from one side of my mid-section, and then the other side. It was moving! Not just moving. It seemed to be stretching, rolling over, maybe yawning. Flashes of *Alien*'s (1979) Giger-infused birth scenes raced through my brain. I turned ghostly white but was also captivated by my writhing mid-section. There was something alive in there. Something big. Something that was eventually going to have to come out.

I know some women like to take a few weeks off before their due date, but I choose to work right up to delivery. Fangoria was a monthly publication at the time, and it was a constant race to get the magazine to press every four weeks.

At forty-one weeks, I was still working full-time at Fango, recording my podcast, hosting Dead Right Horror Pub Trivia in L.A., and attending press screenings. At forty-two weeks I attended the world premiere of the *Evil Dead* (2013) remake. As I was walking into the theater, one of the publicists joked that he hoped I'd go into labor during the movie so they could put out a press release that the film was terrifying enough to cause a Fangoria employee to give birth. But this kid was not moving.

I was getting close to the cut date…literally. At forty-two weeks, the kid had not dropped and was still facing the wrong way, comfortably chilling in breech with no intention of moving. Still nestled deep in my upper abdomen, she had not only impeded my ability to take full breaths and eat a normal meal, there were also moments when I felt little arms exploring. OK, it felt like she was punching my ribs! Plus, she had grown in size to the point where the general consensus with my doctor was that this was going to be a very unpleasant delivery…especially if they had to induce. I lived in a constant state of praying for labor and fearing it. I reached a breaking point and suddenly realized they just needed to get this writhing, stubborn thing out of me.

I had spent the prior nine months fearing the idea of a C-section. They slice you in half, right? They touch your organs, right? By forty-two weeks, my fear of a surgical procedures and scarification were somewhat lessened by the increasingly uncomfortable situation. After finding out I was getting dehydrated and having asthma issues, I scheduled a C-section for 3 p.m. the next day.

Over the next twenty-four hours, I learned more about myself than I did through the entire prior nine months of pregnancy. Faced with an impending gut-slicing, you would think watching gory movies may not be on top of the to-do list. But it was all I wanted to do. That night I watched *Dr. Giggles* (1992) and *Pieces* (1982), relishing in the truly cathartic nature of extreme horror movies. Through these comedic, campy portrayals of carnage, I excised my fears and poked my own mortality. I was going to make it through this. Bastardsssss!

Twelve hours later, I was laying on a bed in triage on the phone with the Fangoria crew, making sure everything was good to go since I was about to be out for a few weeks. I spoke with our editor-in-chief Chris to make certain all ads and graphics were ready for placement. And finally, just before I was about to be wheeled into surgery, I got a call from our president at the time, Tom Defeo, wishing me the best of luck and telling me how a baby would change my entire life.

I had long gathered that natural births were quite a Cronenbergian experience. They'd made us watch birthing videos in our "labor class" at the hospital, and they were far more horrific than most horror films I've seen. There was screaming, and blood, and bits of flesh, and more screaming, and fluids, and what the hell is that surgical instrument, and primal screams of a woman's entire soul being ripped in twain, and more blood, and then a small squirming alien-looking being who was also…screaming.

But I was having a nice controlled C-section. This should be a breeze. It began with the doctor telling me to sit and bend forward while they examined my spine looking for a good place to patch in. I was told they were going to bathe my spinal column in some "feel good" juice so I couldn't move or feel anything. Uhhhh, what? And before I could protest I felt a shot go into the dead center of my lower back. It stung and felt bizarre. Thoughts of the spinal ports from Cronenberg's *eXistenZ* (1999) sprinted through my brain as the world became surreal. My arms went first, then my legs, then the entire rest of my body except for my head became completely and utterly paralyzed.

"I can't move my legs!"

"That's the idea!" my doctor chuckled back.

My doctor knew I worked in horror and spent most of my life watching movies that would make the average movie goers stomachs' churn. She had long joked that childbirth would be a breeze for me because I'd watched so many people be cinematically eviscerated, impaled, and disemboweled. She handled everything from the spinal shunt to explaining the surgery she was about to perform with a perky, cavalier approach. I glanced at the tray table of shining metal tools now positioned just to the left of my head. Some were sharp, some were pointed, some had teeth. One looked like a fucking saw. It was *Dead Ringers* (1988), and I was completely immobilized.

I lay there half exploring and half panicking about this new sensation of being completely paralyzed, simply because the only thing I could do was lie there and exist in my own mind. I was breathing. Air was going in through my mouth and coming back out. But I felt nothing. I could see my chest moving up and down. But I felt none of it. And for the first time in my life I was aware of my own beating heart, and that I could no longer feel it. It had been beating, unnoticed, deep in my chest cavity for thirty-six years, but now that I could no longer feel the constant gentle hum of my continuous biological metronome, I was grossly cognizant of the lack of drumming.

By this time, a white curtain had been constructed across my mid-section, and my doctor was already at work. They were clearly doing something on the other side of the curtain.

"You have great abs" she remarked.

"Excuse me?"

"Your abs. They are really healthy, and you'll have no problem getting them back to normal after this."

It dawned on me then that she was not just looking at my mid-section commenting on my abs. She was looking at my abdominal muscles from the inside! She could see them and was making commentary of my innards. I was rather amused by this thought.

Then I glanced slightly to my right and saw a vat. I could hear suction and saw some type of weird vacuum tubing being moved around by a nurse just beyond the white sheet. But then I saw the vat! About five feet away was a clear, sealed medical vat which was slowly filling with tissue, blood, and other fluids. Oh my god! That was me! That was my insides… slowly filling a clear plastic vat several feet away from my body. And no one seemed even slightly alarmed. They were focused, but cracking jokes; there was jazz music playing.

My distress was suddenly refocused as my doctor informed me it was time to simulate contractions and that I would feel a lot of pressure. Before I could ask "what type of pressure?" a muscle-bound male nurse elbow-dropped on my mid-section. I gasped and suddenly felt like every bit of my guts had been expelled from my belly in one swift jolt.

Then I heard it—crying. A shrill, breathless cry like nothing I had ever heard before.

There she was. My daughter.

She was a tiny, alien-looking goo ball, but she was mine. I had made her. This was and always will be the most ethereal I have ever felt. I still look back in pure astonishment at this moment. It was magic, worth every unpleasant Cronenbergian moment.

Days later, I took my now slightly less alien-looking baby daughter to her first pediatrician's appointment, but by this time I had a whole new concern. My house of horrors.

After a lifetime of horror fandom and many years working in the genre industry, my house was basically one giant scrapbook to everything I loved. Horror posters covered the walls, haunted house accents dotted the rooms. Horror keepsakes, curios, and knick-knacks occupied most premium spaces, not to mention my DVD and books collections which boasted a wide variety of the most frightening and controversial explorations of cinema and literature.

What was I going to do? Eventually this cute little squirmy ball of goo was going to look at the stuff around the house. Would my *Jaws* (1975) poster wreck her for life? Would she later be telling a therapist about how she was never able to use the toilet after she glanced at a copy of *Ghoulies* (1984) on my shelf? Did I need to completely change my house, decor, t-shirt selections, and lifestyle to make sure my daughter grew up "normal?"

I have a feeling most parents go into their first pediatrician appointments with questions about infant sleeping habits, eating schedules, bathing, and basic care needs. My visit was more of a testimonial about all the weird and horrifying stuff I have around my house followed by endless psychology questions about child development and if I was going to mentally wreck her for life. I was prepared to strip my entire house, place everything in my garage, and replace it with nice happy home décor like chevron accent pillows or a "Live Laugh Love" sign. It sounded excruciating and definitely not me, but I would do it for this little squirming, screaming being of pure joy. It's what Moms are supposed to do, right?

The doctor smirked as I prattled wildly, detailing the horrors of my *Cujo* (1983) lobby cards and *Pumpkinhead* (1988) statues. Finally, she cut me off and said, "you're fine."

I'm fine?

"You're totally fine." she said. "Your daughter will tell you if something scares her. And most likely if she has grown up around it from the start, it won't bother her at all. It will just be home. If she tells you something scares her, you ask her why, and then decide how to proceed, but most likely growing up in this environment, she will be just fine."

Even hearing the doctor say this I was not fully convinced, but I stayed they course, and aside from some of my overly sexy exploitation film posters (which still reside in my garage), I left everything as it was. And now seven years later (and also adding my four year old son to the family), neither kid has told me any of the horror stuff around the house scares them. They ask questions. In many cases, they make jokes.

For instance the giant fish on my *Up From the Depths* (1979) poster has been named "Virgil" because one day my daughter told me he needed a name, and that was the first name she could read on the bottom poster credits. Virgil hangs in the dining room, and the kids love to yell at him. Sometimes my son will ask to watch DVDs off the shelf. He is especially fond of *The Return of the Living Dead* (1985) box. I will place it back on the shelf and respond, "not 'til your older," knowing full well this is only making it more tantalizing, and one day he will try to sneak it. I do believe that is how I discovered that very same movie.

The kids are alright.

I have no idea what normal parenting is. My kids definitely seem to know a large amount of trivial information about most iconic movie monsters, and they have already viewed endless adolescent spooky movies like *Monster Squad* (1987), *Jurassic Park* (1993), *Halloweentown*

(1998), and *Hocus Pocus* (1993). My daughter is a little creeped out by scary clowns, but my son finds them fascinating and loves to taunt her with them.

The rest, I'm figuring out as I go. I'm a parent. A horror-loving parent. I'm proud of my horror background, and my kids are too. One of my biggest lessons of parenting—be proud of your passions, your strengths, your knowledge, and your geekiness.

And you were right, Tom. It did change everything.

Fashion and Fear: Where Diamonds, Denim and Decapitation Meet

by Zena Dixon

As you read this, I am most likely talking about one of two things: horror movies or fashion. But if I am really lucky, I am talking about fashion in horror. Often times, this is overlooked by viewers, but not by the artists behind the films. For the wearer, fashion makes you feel. For the observer, it influences your expectations of the wearer. You see the glamour, the elegance, the indifferent, the nonexistent, and the threat. Therefore, fashion is as important in horror than in any other genre.

Let's start with the glamour, and peek at the high fashion knowledge of some top costume designers. The first person that comes to my mind is Erin Benach, known for films such as *A Star is Born* (2018), *Drive* (2011) and *The Host* (2013). But the film that stood out the most for me was the dazzling *The Neon Demon* (2016), directed by Nicolas Winding Refn. Jesse (Elle Fanning) is an aspiring model, new to Los Angeles. Her innocence is soon lost, and we can see her transformation from a modest flowy, spaghetti strap pink dress, to a shimmering, low cut Saint Laurent gown or a blue, strapless Emporio Armani dress. Oftentimes, a woman isn't convincing when she first takes on a new style, but Jesse relishes in the pressure. And from what I've seen, Benach has never failed in enhancing any actor's believability.

There should be no surprise that director Guillermo Del Toro made this article, especially with his Victorian inspired *Crimson Peak* (2015).

He partnered with costumer designer Kate Hawley, who also contributed her skills to *Suicide Squad* (2016) and *Pacific Rim* (2013). On *Crimson Peak*, she excelled at textures and colors, putting Edith Cushing (Mia Wasikowska) in a rich yellow gown with puff shoulders, or a white dress with a puritan collar closing to a long maroon ribbon. I could write a whole article about every costume in this film, but it might rival the *Lord of the Rings* trilogy lengthwise. So, I'll refrain.

Toning down the glamour just a notch, we dive into *The Love Witch* (2016), in which Anna Biller served as the director, music producer, set designer and costume designer. With all of this responsibility, I thought one of those positions would suffer. But I was wrong. Biller dressed Elaine (Samantha Robinson) in different colors, one being a rich pink hat toting large pink flowers. Beneath it, her black hair cascaded down to a pale pink dress against bright red fingernails. With the color choices, you knew you were getting this director's vision wholeheartedly.

Another visionary is Simon Rumley, whose horror film *Fashionista* (2016) featured some great designs, especially for April (Amanda Fuller). She went through a variety of outfits, arriving in one scene in a simple white and blue floral print blouse. But what had me searching online stores for three days with no sleep was not her clothing, but her earrings: blue and about the length and half the width of a pen cap. Though simple, they hung from her ears like icicles, which matched the mood of seeing her husband kissing another woman. In addition to the earrings, I enjoyed April as a fashion fiend. Her obsession with clothing was one I could understand. The smell and feel of fabrics resonated in this film. Being surrounded by textures, the slipperiness of velvet or the thickness of wool, transplants you into another world. Only people capable of your time and attention can take off these prized colors and textures. When they do, they are shedding their armor, only to find a layer of lingerie that hints at the animal they are behind closed doors.

Staying on the topic of glamor and beasts, costume designer Eiko Ishioka ruled the world with her work on *The Cell* (2000), *The Fall* (2006) and *Mirror, Mirror* (2012). But it's her work in Francis Ford Coppola's *Dracula* (1992) that many people first reference as her contribution to high fashion in film, especially having won the Academy Award for Best Costume Design. Taking on a story of this caliber often requires clothes of intricate design. Ishioka, stepping up to the challenge, contrasted the dark set designs with vivacious reds, golds, whites, and peppermint greens. Even with Dracula (Gary Oldman), Ishioka dressed him in a red kabuki robe with gold birds embroidered down the front. A bold and unforeseen move in many viewers opinions.

Two years a later, another vampire film pulsated with high fashion. Neil Jordan's *Interview With the Vampire* (1994) featured Tom Cruise, Brad Pitt, and many other Hollywood actors in extravagant attire from varying time periods. Costume designer Sandy Powell (*Mary Poppins Returns* [2018], *The Departed* [2006]) took us from the vampire Louis (Pitt) in a well-fitted black suit to the beginning of his vampiric existence, during the late Baroque/Rococo style with ruffled collars, lace, and velvets. To see these A-listers in these costumes made me wonder what the Oscars would have been like during this period.

If I attended the Oscars during that time, I would hire Theoni V. Aldredge as my stylist. She established the costume designs for *Ghostbusters* (1984), *Addams Family Values* (1993) and *The First Wives Club* (1996), and won the Oscar for *The Great Gatsby* (1974). I was first introduced to Aldredge's work in *Eyes of Laura Mars* (1978). Directed by Irvin Kershner, this film follows Laura Mars (Faye Dunaway), a famous fashion photographer whose eyes often see the murderous activity of a serial killer. While the story sticks with you, I often find myself fantasizing about Laura's dark orange top with the ruffled collar and sleeves, her air of glamour as she strived to explain her visions to Detective John Neville (Tommy Lee Jones). Likewise, who could forget the burgundy top and matching scarf she wore, frantic but fashionable in the woods. Oh, the delightful designs of the seventies!

But what about the 1960s? Well, for that, I reference Mario Bava's *Blood and Black Lace* (1964). One of the many reasons I love this film is costume designer Tina Grani, who also served in the same capacity on *Black Sabbath* (1963), partnering again with Mario Bava, who served as cinematographer. In *Blood and Black Lace*, Grani conjured numerous styles for several different personalities, but my go-to design is Countess Christina Como (Eva Bartok) in all black, accessorized with an off-center belt and a necklace that hung down both sides of her neck—but didn't connect. I had never seen anything like this necklace before, one that could easily fall from the shoulder, which forced the wearer to walk with grace. I actually thought that this was the dark magic in the movie, and I wanted to know what master she served in order to get a necklace like that.

From the excitement of glamour, we go to the ingeniously simple nature of elegance. We start with Dario Argento's *Phenomena* (1985), starring Jennifer Connelly as Jennifer Corvino. Her fashion sense was often subtle but effective, making her seem like a sagacious young girl. Her iconic white shirt and white skirt with matching white socks into—yes—black shoes left many women shivering in fear. Even though this was a horror movie with honest scares, I was more afraid of that outfit. I hope to one day be brave enough to wear white socks and black shoes. Truthfully, I guess you have to be brave and special to be dressed by Giorgio Armani. I was shocked when I later discovered his hands were on the costumes of this film. It's like the world came together for me.

Phenomena also showed me that a charm could be worn every day, and may even serve as a piece that defines you for a time period. The Headmistress (Dalila Di Lazzaro) wore an elegant silver charm around her neck, ornamenting her plain, white forward-point collared shirt, or her black dress with padded shoulders.

Stepping from the women for a bit, we jump to a man, a quite unusual man by the name of Patrick Bateman (Christian Bale) in Mary Harron's *American Psycho* (2000). His decorative ties, gold watch, forward-point collared shirts, Valentino Couture suits, Oliver Peoples eyeglasses, and not a single hair out of place intrigued us. But his obsession for these things left us relieved that this was a character and not our co-worker. Your believability and unbelievability was distorted after this film, because a trip through a city or an office building often presented you with a Patrick Bateman look alike.

Staying on believability, it's not hard to believe that another Guillermo Del Toro film would make this article. *Pan's Labyrinth* (2006) can be described as elegant dress-wise, simply because of the time period: 1944 Falangist Spain. Sure, we can acknowledge Ofelia (Ivana Baquero) in her wool peacoat and black tam hat. But what most people recall is her green hairbow and matching green skater dress, rising to a Peter Pan collar beneath a white pinafore tied at the back. This take on the *Alice in Wonderland* attire left many people yearning for this outfit.

Now, we jump from Del Toro to James Wan, and reminisce over his characters Ed and Lorraine Warren (Patrick Wilson and Vera Farmiga) in *The Conjuring* (2013). Many people remember their subtle yet elegant clothing choices. A stand-out scene takes place in a lecture hall, where both Warrens are in well-groomed attire: Ed in a long-collared shirt, tie, and dark buttonless cotton vest with a suit jacket boasting large lapels, while Lorraine maintained a simple but approachable style with circular earrings drawing the viewer to her smile above a turtleneck. Paranormal researchers are often perceived as a hoax, and at times were, but Ed and

Lorraine's appearance gave you the sense that they had something worth hearing. Even when they entered homes, they maintained their professional appearance. Pointing his shotgun microphone to potential ghost chatter, Ed could be seen in a black dress shirt under a fitted cotton sweater. Lorraine dressed for agility, wearing a white dress shirt with an open, brown vest. This look was perfected by costume designer Kristin M. Burke, known for *Insidious* (2010), *Lights Out* (2016) and much more.

A different form of elegance can be seen in Katt Shea's *Poison Ivy* (1992), starring Drew Barrymore, who by this point in her career had become somewhat of a style icon. As Ivy in the film, Barrymore pulled off anything. What she introduced many women to is that a black leather jacket can be versatile. She even wore the jacket over a bohemian combination, a red long sleeve crop top and colorful skirt. Many women didn't consider a leather jacket an everyday thing, but Barrymore made us realize otherwise. Then, as a bolder step into fashion divinity, she appeared in an oversized red coat over a white shirt and bodycon, black and red mini-skirt. I adored the fights and freaky things she did while also appearing runway ready.

Ha Nguyen, costume designer for films such as *Super 8* (2011), *Mortal Kombat* (1995), and *The Mask* (1994), is no stranger to dressing actors for extreme situations. But it was her simple elegance for Maximillian (Eddie Murphy) in Wes Craven's *Vampire in Brooklyn* (1995) that resonates with me the most. Naturally, Maximillian was cloaked in a black trench coat like most modern vampires, but Nguyen embellished it with a decorative black and orange button-down shirt with a mandarin collar. Furthermore, seeing the different versions of New Yorkers in the 90s easily transported me back to my time in Brooklyn, though with a much darker ambience under Nguyen's artistry.

Possession (1981), from director and writer Andrzej Zulawksi, also featured some of the best outfits for men and women, this time taking us to Berlin. Mark (Sam Neill) supplied the sex appeal in his gray suit, over a gray collared shirt and dark gray tie. For me, this was one of my first introductions to men outside of the casual black suits. Anna/Helen (Isabel Adjani) resonated, whether in all black or all white. However, it was her bluish dress with the button-down back that most viewers remember. I remember it because the dress was just the dress—no accessories, no embellishments—almost like the dress was as alone as she was at that moment. Others remember it because this is the dress she wore during her possession scene in the train station.

Dario Argento hits the list again, this time with his own possession classic *Suspiria* (1977). With costume designer Pierangelo Cicoletti, whom Argento partnered with years later on *Tenebre* (1982), *Suspiria* resonates with costumes that often match the set design. In one iconic scene, Suzy Bannion (Jessica Harper) wears a long red dress and walks into a white and red room that, instead of overpowering her, oddly accentuates her. This allowed me to realized that there is an extraordinary opportunity to make a statement with any outfit. If I'm feeling like I want to reign at an event, I will research the establishment and attempt to compliment the decor. People may unknowingly get a sense that you have some sort of ownership of the location. Additionally, I did notice that Cicoletti dressed some of the cast in white or black. This enabled the set design and lighting to receive the attention, while keeping characters visible to viewers.

With all these fashion designs, I still feel that the 50s had some of the coolest and most sophisticated styles. I often watch Gene Fowler Jr.'s *I Was a Teenage Werewolf* (1957) primarily for the wardrobe. Arlene Logan (Yvonne Lime) was my favorite in that striped dress, flared at the bottom, and three rows of pearls fitted to her neck. But it was that jacket, open except for the button at the collar, that made me scream, sort of like Adjani in *Possession*.

We've pinpointed examples of glamor and elegance, but now it's time for the casual or withdrawn characters in fashion. I know most people loved *The Guest* (2014) by Adam Wingard. Yes, the story was exhilarating with a beautiful yet unstable soldier (Dan Stevens) coming to the house, but what engrossed me more were the outfits of Anna Peterson (Maika Monroe). Even her restaurant attire, with the broad yellow collar over the baby blue dress, black knee-high socks down to the black combat boots, and the oh-my-lord-is-that-yellow-shoe-string touch made me cry in my closet because I could have dressed much better during my waitressing years. Her outfit singlehandedly turned that mediocre restaurant into a vintage rock establishment. But what has been driven deeper into my mind is the black and white dress with the skull covering almost sixty percent of it. And then she had the fearlessness to wear what looked like a garter belt underneath. I know who I'm going to be for the rest of my life. Yes, her. Monroe always excels at playing a girl who stands out with style without being an attention seeker. Furthermore, costume designer Kathleen Detoro knew exactly how to achieve this look, and typically triumphs with introverted characters, having created the look for characters on *Breaking Bad*.

From here we go to McG's *The Babysitter* (2017), which featured costumes that served the purpose of defining the characters. Aside from straightforward personalities, generic names and typical dialogue, *The Babysitter* didn't avoid dressing the character in typical costumes. For example, Bee (Samara Weaving) was the cool, casual girl in jean shorts and a white tee under an open, long sleeve green button-down shirt. The outfit conveyed a girl who was cool enough to get a party started anywhere, but could remain lowkey in a casual environment. She was sexy when she wanted to be, especially during the energetic scene at the pool with her red swimsuit. Cole (Judah Lewis) was the young boy Bee babysat. His conservative personality showed through his white collared, button-down shirt and burgundy pants. Even when Bee and Cole stood side-by-side on the front porch waving bye to his parents, you could clearly see the influence they had on each other. But things went to hell when her friends arrived to Cole's home. Allison (Bella Thorne) was unmistakable as the airhead cheerleader with a bright yellow top, matching skirt, and ribbon in her hair. Max (Robbie Amell), the jock, beamed constantly in a jean jacket, white t-shirt, and big belt buckle over black jeans. Rounding out the crew was jokester John (Andrew Bachelor) in a gray sweater with a white t-shirt peeking from the bottom, and artist Sonya (Hana Mae Lee) with a white long sleeve sweater, black skirt, oversized bowtie and tam hat.

Often times, multiple key pieces of clothing help you define a character. But every now and then, you come across a film where there is one key piece that makes you remember the whole film. In director Coralie Fargeat's *Revenge* (2017), Jen (Matilda Anna Ingrid Lutz) wore a pair of neon pink star earrings. These earrings were with her throughout the entire film, whether drinking a beer or returning bullets in a gun fight. Furthermore, when the earrings got a little dirty, these beauties still glowed, even inspiring the color for the movie's title card. This let me know that one small piece of attire can influence something much larger.

This level of accessorizing can also be seen in Jaromil Jires' *Valerie and Her Week of Wonders* (1970). While costume designer Eva Lackingerová (*Prodloužený cas* [1984], *Catherine and Her Children* [1975]) dressed the supporting cast primarily in black and white with few accessories, a pair of beautiful, gold, lantern-shaped earrings distinguished the main character Valerie (Jaroslava Schallerová). The sight of these earrings has stuck with me for decades.

I remember watching *Valerie and Her Week of Wonders* in 1996, the same year director Andrew Fleming introduced us to the most unique four witches to ever hit the big screen. And it was costume designer Deborah Everton (*Halloween H20: 20 Years Later* [1998], *The Abyss* [1989]) that created the looks for this quartet. *The Craft* (1996) familiarized us with Nancy Downs (Fairuza Balk) in a mid-thigh skirt, combat boots, and an upturned collar framing her gorgeous face, which succumbed to heavy eyeliner. Then we met the radiant Rochelle (Rachel True) in preppy black attire with rolled up sleeves and big collars. Bonnie (Neve Campbell) served as the deeper introvert, hidden behind baggier clothes, oversized jackets and ankle length dresses. Last addition to the group was Sarah Bailey (Robin Tunney), who appeared to be a mixture of all of the other girls with a hint of valley girl.

Sticking with witchcraft, many people remember Roman Polanski's *Rosemary's Baby* (1968), mainly for Rosemary. I remember it more for her pregnancy attire. Costume designer Anthea Sylbert (*The Heartbreak Kid* [1972], *Chinatown* [1974]) introduced me to the fun outfits a pregnant woman can have. As a child, I dreaded the pregnant life because of the fashion around me: the ankle length nightgowns with either one solid color and no design, or the simple vertical stripes similar to a sad clown costume. But to see Rosemary (Mia Farrow) in her baby blue nightgown, especially with decorative white lace stitching around the buttons, let young me know that pregnancy didn't mean dull fashion options. Then again, even before pregnancy, Rosemary was a fashion powerhouse. That all-white dress and off-white purse during their home hunting was stimulating. However, the outfit that still whispers to my wallet is the checkered peacoat with the rounded collar, mid-high black skirt and fishnet stockings.

Another film that stands out for casual fashion is Roger Corman's *Cat People* (1942). Certainly, high fashion existed in this film, especially from the mind of costume designer Marjorie Corso, who also offered her gifts to *Tales of Terror* (1962) and *The Haunted Palace* (1963). In *Cat People*, Corso delivered attractive, high-end designs for lead characters Irena Dubrovna Reed (Simone Simon), Oliver Reed (Kent Smith), and Alice Moore (Jane Rudolph). But my attention was stuck on the casual ensemble of Minnie (Theresa Harris). Though her waitress role was small, Minnie radiated in that dress with the small black bow in the front contrasting the huge white bow in the back of her apron. I know the focus was supposed to be on the main characters in that dining scene, but Minnie moving in the background made me want to find out more about her, especially because I never looked that spicy in a waitress outfit.

Lastly, we must acknowledge some of the more menacing, yet still attractive, fashion choices in horror. What immediately comes to my mind are the Cenobites from Clive Barker's *Hellraiser* (1987). These man-shaped creatures are supposed to be threatening, especially being a religious sect from Hell. But most people can't deny that Pinhead's ensemble leans more on the sexy side. That fitted, black leather outfit, with the cutouts revealing parts of Pinhead's smooth chest and stomach, made this Cenobite hint that the people of Hell might have some fashion sense. And it would be hard not to, with costume designer Joanna Johnston styling you. Johnston is one of the greats in the industry, responsible for the costume designs in *War of the Worlds* (2005), *The Sixth Sense* (1999), and *Death Becomes Her* (1992).

While Pinhead (Doug Bradley) revealed a little skin, we must travel to Michael Duggan's *Mausoleum* (1983) for more. Susan Walker Farrell (Bobbie Bresee) didn't appear threatening when she was out in public, donning conservative ensembles such as her white sweater with the cowl collar falling over her brown coat. But it was her lingerie that made you feel like she knew what she wanted—and was going to get it. When she opened the door in her silk, mauve pink corselette with the lace trimming and matching coat, I knew the delivery boy was in trouble. To make matters worse, she had numerous revealing ensembles that men couldn't deny. If the mauve one didn't do the trick, the white one did. This revealed the importance of lingerie for me and my future on this planet.

Continuing with threatening ensembles, we arrive at Tim Burton's 2007 hit *Sweeney Todd: The Demon Barber of Fleet Street*. Sweeney Todd (Johnny Depp) is a barber who clearly looks like he would slit your throat; however, clients still sat in his chair with a smile. With his wingtip-collared white shirt, shabby double-breasted vest, black gloves, high-waisted pinstripe pants and black dress shoes, Sweeney Todd has become the inspiration for many costumes during the Halloween season. Even his brown leather belt served a different purpose, not holding up his pants, but supporting his sharp, signature razors. This showcases the importance of accessibility in fashion.

Obviously, fashion is alive and well in horror. My disappointment is that I am unable to address it all here. But what I hope we agree on is that fashion in film helps define the character. It draws us closer to them, and gives a physical reference on how to become them. At times, it even provides a muse for you to create the person you ultimately want to become yourself. The next time you are in need of some fashion inspiration, don't hesitate to look to the horror genre. It will be waiting for you—though I can't promise it will be with safe intentions.

Food and Horror: An Unexpected Pairing

by Sarah Ann Stubbs

Food. We need to eat and drink to survive. It's something that connects all of us. As someone who has developed a career as a food writer and content creator with an emphasis in pop culture, it's hard not to notice some things when it comes to the convergence of food and pop culture.

Much like other biological functions, most movie genres tend to ignore the necessity of eating—or even food for that matter. Of course, there are exceptions; there always are. Fantasy tends to come to the forefront when one thinks of a feast scene or use of food to further the story. A great example of this is the *Harry Potter* series. After watching the films, it was hard not to be jealous of meals in The Great Hall.

So what does this have to do with horror? It probably comes as a surprise (or maybe not) that the horror genre also uses food and restaurants to move a plot along. This isn't even taking into account movies that feature killer foods (what I will refer to as "foodie features"). Let's be real for a second and acknowledge the fact that two popular sub-genres of horror involve creatures who are really just hungry (vampires and zombies).

Not including the aforementioned vampire and zombie subgenres, there are a couple of areas where food comes into play in horror movies. They are:

- Foodie Features
- Feast Scenes
- General Instances of Food Being Used as a Plot Device
- Cannibalism

Let's dig in and chew the fat (so to speak) about why food and horror is the perfect recipe for fun.

Foodie Features

Creature Features have been around basically as long as cinema has been a thing. One of the earliest Creature Features, *The Golem*, was released in 1915. However, we're talking about food so we are more concerned with "foodie features".

So what the heck is a "foodie feature?" Well, think of a Creature Feature but as with a recipe, substitute the creature with a killer food! Foodie Features tend to be a bit sillier than your standard horror film. After all, how can you take a movie where food is attacking people seriously? Interestingly enough, these films seem to spawn sequels so there must be something to them.

Some of the most well-known "foodie features" include:

- *The Stuff* (1985) – *The Stuff* is a Larry Cohen film that features a killer low-calorie dessert made up of an organism that destroys people's brains, turning them into zombies. It's unfortunate that this film never got a sequel when other less deserving Foodie Features have.

- *Attack of the Killer Tomatoes* (1978) – Perhaps the most notable (and closest to my heart) of the Foodie Features is *Attack of the Killer Tomatoes*. It has three sequels: *Return of the Killer Tomatoes!* (1988), *Killer Tomatoes Strike Back!* (1990), and *Killer Tomatoes Eat France!* (1991). It even had a children's cartoon created after it. Honestly, growing up I had no idea that the cartoon was based on an actual movie. Not only that, but it also had video games and comics based off the original movie. Murmurs of a new sequel have been abuzz for years but nothing has happened.

- *Poultrygeist: Night of the Dead Chicken* (2006) – *Poultrygeist: Night of the Dead Chicken* comes from the folks over at Troma, so you can expect a wild ride. All you really need to know about this movie is that it involves a fast food chain built on a burial ground and zombie chickens. Enough said.

- *Gingerdead Man* (2005) – Much like *Poultrygeist*, *Gingerdead Man* is a movie full of camp, this time coming from Charles Band and Full Moon Entertainment. The premise of the film is a gingerbread man made of sugar, spice, and a serial killer's ashes. Much like *Attack of the Killer Tomatoes*, it has spawned several sequels (*Gingerdead Man 2: Passion of the Crust* [2008] and *Gingerdead Man 3: Saturday Night Cleaver* [2011]) as well as the off-shoot *Gingerdead Man Vs. Evil Bong* (2013). Also, in the same vein as *Tomatoes*, it had its own comic as well.

- *ThanksKilling* (2009) – Who doesn't love a low budget holiday horror movie? Have you noticed a trend in Foodie Features yet? Their names don't leave many questions as to what they are about. In *ThanksKilling*, a possessed turkey picks off five college kids during their Thanksgiving break. The film was shot on a $3,500 budget[1] and also had a follow-up sequel, *ThanksKilling 3* (2012).

One would think that there would be far more of these types of movies. Alas, there isn't much high budget hype for killer food. That is to say, the studios don't seem too interested in investing money to make this type of horror film. In fact, all of the above mentioned movies were either given a small theatrical release or were released straight to home video.

Feast Scenes

One of the most universal experiences we have as social creatures is dining around a table. Feast scenes are an illustration of this in film and literature. For the sake of definition, I will be using the term to discuss the use of a dining or restaurant scene to further the story.

Within horror movies, feast scenes are a bit different than in fantasy type fiction. They may not be a large feast in a traditional sense of the word but are rather a gathering of people where the storytelling happens

---

1. Rome, Emily. "Murderous Turkey Coming to LMU in Alumni's Film Sequel." *Los Angeles Loyolan*, 17 Nov. 2011, www.laloyolan.com/arts_and_entertainment/film_tv/murderous-turkey-coming-to-lmu-in-alumni-s-film-sequel/article_0f07a57c-0ff8-11e1-879a-001a4bcf6878.html.

during a dining scene. In some instances, for example, *Psycho* (1960), the scene between Marion and Norman in the back office of the Bates Motel could be considered a feast scene as it is where we learn a bit about both characters and their motivations while they share a small meal of sandwiches.

Among the more traditional feast scenes are:

- *A Quiet Place* (2018) – In *A Quiet Place*, during the dinner scene we learn about the day to day life of the Abbott family and how they interact now that they are unable to speak or make loud noises. It also serves to illustrate the family dynamic.

- *Alien* (1979) – *Alien* has one of the most recognizable feast scenes. As the crew of the Nostromo gathers to eat and celebrate Kane's awakening before returning to stasis, the Xenomorph makes its first appearance as it bursts out of Kane's chest. This scene sets the tone for the rest of the film.

- *House of 1000 Corpses* (2003) – In his first foray into movies, Rob Zombie's *House of 1000 Corpses* uses the concept of a feast scene perfectly. When Bill, Jerry, Denise, and Mary get stranded on the side of the road and end up dining with the Firefly family, they learn that they may have gotten themselves into something they shouldn't have. The discomfort they feel in this scene is palpable.

- *IT* (1990) – In the *IT* TV mini-series, The Loser's Club returns to Derry and celebrates their reunion with dinner in a Chinese restaurant. At the close of their dinner, they are terrorized by Pennywise via fortune cookies. Not only does this scene deliver some scares, but it also further develops and showcases the friendship of The Losers.

There are a few movies that have important but low key feast scenes. Like *Psycho*, the feast scenes in these films are shorter or have fewer people. However, they still share vital information or character development equal to films with longer scenes.

- *Jaws (1975)* – Unlike most of the films discussed above, *Jaws* actually has two feast scenes. The first is when Matt Hooper comes over to the Brody home to meet with Martin and they discuss the fact that the shark that was caught was not, in fact, the shark terrorizing Amity. The second is aboard the Orca when Quint, Hooper, and Brody are sitting around the table drinking beers and comparing battle scars. Both scenes subtly deliver important character development while moving the story forward. *Jaws 3 (1983)* also has a scene in a bar that somewhat fits within the parameters of a feast scene.

- *Terrifier (2017)* – I almost didn't add *Terrifier*, but the pizza parlor scene comes pretty close to being a feast scene of sorts. It further introduces us to the two female leads as well as Art the Clown. What is most unsettling about this scene is that you know Art is bad news but his actions seem silly and you almost let your guard down—at least until he gets up to go to the restroom.

- *American Werewolf of London (1981)* – In *American Werewolf of London*, the scene at The Slaughtered Lamb early on in the film warns our main character of things to come. In true horror movie fashion, David doesn't listen (it wouldn't be much of a movie if he did) and is attacked, thus leading him to become the titular creature.

There are other movies that have scenes that could possibly be construed as feast scenes but the ones discussed are definitely the most prominent (or in the case of *The Texas Chain Saw Massacre* [1974] were omitted due to fitting in another category). At the end of the day, the feast scene's purpose is to give an audience a sense of relatability to the characters on screen.

General Instances of Food Being Used as a Plot Device

Aside from being based on killer food or having a feast scene, there are numerous horror movies that use food or restaurants as a plot device. These instances won't necessarily do the same amount of storytelling as a feast scene but they prominently feature food nonetheless. It can be as simple as events taking place in a restaurant or other food-oriented location, a specific food item, or even a plot featuring an overeater.

A restaurant is a pretty common setting for movie scenes to take place in, and horror movies are no exception. Movies like the above mentioned *American Werewolf in London*, *Terrifier*, and *IT* all have scenes that take place in restaurants. Additionally, you have movies like *Jason Goes to Hell: The Final Friday* (1993), a personal favorite, and *Blood and Donuts* (1995) which have prominent restaurant scenes (The diner in *Jason Goes to Hell* and the donut shop in *Blood and Donuts*). Slightly different yet in the same vein, *The Blair Witch Project* (1999) and *Book of Shadows: Blair Witch 2* (2000) both include scenes in grocery stores which involve both food elements and story development.

There are many unique uses of food in horror. Food can be affected by the supernatural like David's rice and noodles that turn into maggots and worms in *The Lost Boys* (1987) or the steak that crawls across the counter in *Poltergeist* (1982). Anthology films pertaining to Halloween like *Tales of Halloween* (2015) and *Trick 'R Treat* (2007) obviously feature heavy candy consumption and stories. However, *Trick 'R Treat* also showcases food as a weapon (Sam's candy bar shiv). Another film that does this is *Killer Klowns from Outer Space* (1988) which has weaponized popcorn and ray guns that turn people into cotton candy. Finally, there are specific food items that are important to characters within the film. Examples include Charlie's love of chocolate and her nut allergy in *Hereditary* (2018), hard boiled eggs and key lime pie in *The Shape of Water* (2017), and gormeh sabzi in *Imitation Girl* (2017).

Thinner (1996) is unique in its use of food because the entire movie is based on a theme of gluttony. When discussing the book the film was based on, Stephen King noted, "It has a funny subtext about eating. It's about how everybody's eating, everywhere, all the time. It's about how we look, how we look at ourselves."[2] In fact, King wrote the book after being told he needed to lose weight. The film's ending is a bit of a happier (if you can call it that) ending than the book.

As mentioned earlier, food can be used to help an audience identify or connect with what's going on in the movie they're viewing. We've all had a favorite food or can identify with the frustration of trying to lose

---

2. "The Works of Richard Bachman." *The Washington Post*, WP Company, www.washingtonpost.com/archive/lifestyle/1985/04/09/the-works-of-richard-bachman/69225339-92e0-46ee-a66e-b503e4700e92/?utm_term=.a16741cd0282.

weight. It's these things that really take a movie watching experience to the next level.

CANNIBALISM

I'd be amiss if I didn't discuss the cannibalism sub-genre. It is, in essence, the ultimate taboo. Whereas feast scenes create a sense of relatability, cannibalism flips it on its head. After all, what's more terrifying than humans eating other humans without the excuse of being undead? The 1970s and 1980s saw the biggest amount of growth in this sub-genre. The films primarily came from Italian filmmakers, with *Cannibal Holocaust* (1980) being perhaps the most controversial due to its excessive gore and depictions of real animal cruelty.

The 1980s brought a few films into the cannibalism sub-genre that were a bit campier and more humorous than the Italian imports. Movies like *Motel Hell* (1980), *Microwave Massacre* (1979), and *Parents* (1989) showed the "softer" side of cannibalism. The tone and realism of these films was much more lighthearted and comical than their Italian predecessors.

Somewhere in between the serious and the campy lies *The Texas Chain Saw Massacre* franchise. The first entry into the series is very gritty and serious. However, each sequel that follows delivers more and more campiness. Sadly, in terms of cannibalism, each film seems to focus on it less and less. *The Texas Chain Saw Massacre* can actually also fit in the Feast Scene category. The dinner scene is one of the most intense and uncomfortable scenes in a horror film. As a viewer, you feel as much confusion and fear as the final girl Sally Hardesty (portrayed by Marilyn Burns).

Cannibalism has even made its way to television. Shows such as *Alfred Hitchcock Presents* ("Specialty of the House," 1959) and *Tales from the Crypt* ("What's Cookin'," 1992) have taken a stab at cannibalism. *The Twilight Zone* also had an episode ("To Serve Man," 1962) that touches on cannibalism—or rather the idea of it. Even *The Simpsons* has gotten in on the fun in their "Treehouse of Horror" episodes. *The X-Files* had an episode with a cannibalism theme ("Our Town," 1995). Executive producer Frank Spotnitz was inspired to write the episode after thinking of cannibalism occurring at a chicken processing plant, which he thought was absolutely vile. He even went as far as to name the characters after real-life cannibals. *Hannibal* (based on the character from Thomas Harris' novels *Red Dragon*, *The Silence of the Lambs*, *Hannibal*, and *Hannibal Rising*) saw quite a bit of popularity during its run from 2013 to 2015, even inspiring its own cookbook, *Feeding Hannibal*.

More recently, films like *Green Inferno* (2013), *Bone Tomahawk* (2015), and *Raw* (2016), along with remakes of *The Texas Chain Saw Massacre* series in the early 2000s, as well as a sequel (*Texas Chainsaw 3D*) in 2013 and a prequel (*Leatherface*) in 2017 have brought cannibalism back to the genre. So why is cannibalism making a comeback? Well, it could be that with society becoming more technologically advanced, the notion of something as primal as cannibalism is terrifying. It also could be as simple as the cyclical nature of movie genres to use various themes, especially when the market isn't saturated with that sub-genre.

At the end of the day, food is a part of our daily lives. Genres that choose to ignore that tend to suffer from a level of inauthenticity that you probably can't explain offhand. You might not recognize it as such, but there is something to be said for adding something as simple as food to connect the audience to what they are watching. The next time you're watching any of the above movies, pay closer attention to the food and the role it plays. Like a meal made with quality ingredients, you'll enjoy it that much more.

I'm Your Biggest Fan—Horror and Fandom

The X-Files, the Scully Effect, and the #metoo Movement

by Alyse Wax

THE X-FILES HAS BEEN one of my favorite TV shows ever since it premiered in 1993. I was thirteen years old, and Agent Dana Scully was a huge inspiration to me. Brilliant, beautiful, and courageous, she taught me that it was okay to be intelligent, to speak my mind, and to not be intimidated by men. She was the first female character I saw on television that wasn't flirting with her male partner (at first) and was more worried about her career than finding a man who would marry her. I even briefly considered a career in the FBI–until I learned that the X-Files wasn't a real division, and I couldn't hunt aliens and monsters. Instead, the show is what inspired me to be a writer.

It seems that in 2018, with the second revival season (Season 11) and the rise of the #metoo movement, fans and critics are going back and reexamining the series. A lot of people seem to come to the conclusion that Scully was treated poorly (which she was—but so was Mulder) and are reconsidering her role as a feminist icon—or at least reconsidering series creator Chris Carter's relevancy in her creation.

A brief refresher on the show for those who are not as obsessive as I am. Special Agent Dana Scully (Gillian Anderson), a medical doctor who felt she could make a bigger difference in the FBI, is sent to "spy" on the brilliant thorn in the Bureau's side, Special Agent Fox Mulder (David Duchovny). Mulder's younger sister, Samantha, was abducted by aliens when they were kids, and he has been obsessed with finding her. He discovered the X-Files—a dumping ground for the files dealing with aliens, monsters, and other unexplainable crimes—and thought that the answer to his sister's disappearance could be found there. Scully is a skeptic. If she doesn't have hardcore science to back up things she has seen with her own eyes, she doesn't believe they are real. They are often aided by their boss, Assistant Director Walter Skinner (Mitch Pileggi). Mixed in with monster-of-the-week episodes are what are called "mytharc" episodes, episodes that contribute to a deep, conspiracy-laden mythology. At its simplest, the mytharc of *The X-Files* revolved around the idea that a shadow government was working on creating alien/human hybrids in order to prepare for colonization by aliens. This effort was led by the Cigarette Smoking Man (William B. Davis), a nameless goon with deep ties within the government.

That Reveal

The furor around the Season 11 premiere seems to be where this reevaluation of the show was born. Cigarette Smoking Man (CSM) revealed that he was the father of William, the child Scully birthed at the end of Season 8 (despite Scully having been declared infertile several years earlier). In the closing minutes of "My Struggle III," CSM revealed to Skinner that he "impregnated [Scully] with science." When Skinner asked who is William's father, CSM's response: "I am. William is my son." Flashbacks were shown from the Season 7 episode "En Ami" in which Scully agrees to accompany CSM on a trip to recover what he claimed to be a cure for cancer. While on this trip (during which Scully remains highly suspicious and untrusting of CSM), she woke in a strange bed, wearing pajamas that she hadn't been wearing the night before. Scully accused CSM of drugging her. In the footage shown during "My Struggle III," CSM is given a line about his housekeeper changing her clothes. This line was *not* in the original episode, nor is a housekeeper ever seen.

This is a shocking revelation. While William's paternity was never *explicitly* confirmed in the series, it was widely believed that Mulder was the father. Both Scully and Mulder operated under this assumption. He was the only person that she slept with in at least three years, and they are *soulmates*. The term "shipper"[1] was literally created for Mulder and Scully.

---

1. Shippers are a rabid subset of any fanbase who pine for two specific characters to hook up. In 1993, when *The X-Files* began, fans instantly picked up on the chemistry between Scully and Mulder, and those who wanted the pair to hook up were initially called "relationshippers." It was shortened to "R'shippers," which eventually became shippers, shipping, and "to ship."

Fans couldn't imagine another outcome. Plus, executive producer Frank Spotnitz blatantly stated the baby was Mulder's. In *Writing the X-Files* by Jason Davis, Spotnitz says:

> "We knew it was going to be Mulder's kid. We planted a moment in the episode that Gillian Anderson wrote and directed ["all things"], which people could look back on and realize *that* was the night they conceived."

In the same interview, Spotnitz admits that when they did tell the audience that it was Mulder's baby, it was so ambiguous that people still weren't sure. He was frequently asked if it was Mulder's baby. "Yes, it is Mulder's baby," he says.

I recently interviewed William B. Davis, the actor who plays CSM, and he believes that it was his sperm used to create William. "I presume I am biologically his father," he told me. Of course, he also admitted that he didn't discuss this particular plot point with series creator Chris Carter. "I don't think we talked about that. I just rolled with that... I have no inside information as to how it developed." As the writer of the episode "En Ami," Davis also assured me that medical rape was not part of the original intent of that episode, and he had not planned some elaborate long-game. "Well, I'd like to say it was, but no. In fact, very little in *The X-Files* is a very long-simmering plan. Most of it is, 'Oh, well, look at that! Maybe we can do blah blah.'" Interestingly, Carter said, in an interview with *Entertainment Weekly*[2], that he had had this planned since Season 7.

I came up with a whole theory about this reveal. It wasn't that CSM is the biological father of William; he just monkeyed with the computer chip in Scully's neck which gave her back her fertility. The chip was given to her during her Season 2 abduction, and has proved to have an effect on her health. Removing it gave her cancer; replacing it sent her cancer into remission. Two episodes after "En Ami," Scully and Mulder have sex for the first time.

I thought that maybe this was the fangirl in me, trying to make sense of a totally worthless plot point. But then I rewatched "Existence," the Season 8 finale in which Scully gives birth. It included this line from Knowle Rohrer (a minor and ultimately unimportant character):

---

2. https://ew.com/tv/2018/01/03/x-files-creator-season-11-premiere-interview/

> "Six years ago, Agent Scully was taken in a military operation staged as an abduction. They put a chip in the back of her neck to monitor her. It was also used to make her pregnant with the first organic version of that same super-soldier."

The chip was *used to make her pregnant*. Last I checked, even in *The X-Files*, you still need sperm for that to happen. As far as I am concerned, this is irrefutable evidence—Scully levels of evidence—that CSM only made it *possible* for her to become pregnant. He didn't impregnate her himself.

Chris Carter himself seems to be unsure of his own thoughts about William's paternity. In the *EW* interview, he says, "[CSM is] the figurative father if he's not the actual father." This I can agree with. It is what he says next that I cannot agree with: "He didn't rape Scully. He impregnated her with science." That is still rape. Whether he physically impregnated Scully or merely made her fertile, the fact that he did so without her permission is medical rape.

Though I may have justified this garbage plot point in my own head, it has angered many fans of the show—and with good reason. Why would Chris Carter do this? Mulder and Scully don't find out about this until the final minutes of the final episode. Nothing in the course of the season is at all affected by this news. Carter claims "it adds to the characters in an interesting emotional way." But fans don't need any more "interesting emotions" with Mulder and Scully. They stuck around for seven years, waiting for them to go to bed together. They stuck around through the mystery pregnancy and Scully giving the baby up for adoption (for William's safety). They stuck around during Mulder and Scully's off-screen breakup before Season 10. In Season 11, we got to watch the pair fall back in love with one another—all while fighting some impressively terrifying monsters-of-the-week.

Some fans seem to feel as though Chris Carter went with this twist simply to fuck with them. In the very early seasons of *The X-Files*, Carter frequently said in interviews that Mulder and Scully were strictly platonic. As the conspiracy goes, Carter didn't count on the off-the-chart chemistry between Duchovny and Anderson, and the characters eventually became romantic towards the end of the series as a way of giving in to fan pressure. Many fans seem to think that this "who's the daddy" plot device was Carter's way of "getting back" at the fans for "pressuring" him to turn the couple romantic. (Sadly, this is one of the saner conspiracy theories.)

"Never attribute to malice that which is adequately explained by stupidity," a quote from computer programmer Robert J. Hanlon, is the quote I prefer to think of when it comes to Chris Carter. I do not think he was trying to "stick it" to the fandom, nor was he jealous of Scully (as another conspiracy theory goes). I think this is just another case of a straight white man who hasn't adapted to the #metoo era. There was no vendetta here. It is merely that he has never faced criticism of this sort; he has never had to think about things like rape or medical rape. He has never written a high-profile show in such a "woke" era.

I do, however, think that this was an incredibly tone-deaf plot point, compounded by an even worse response: "He didn't rape Scully. He impregnated her with science." I honestly believe that this plot twist would not have been met with quite so much vitriol if Carter had simply said, "Cigarette Smoking Man has always been a bad guy. He does bad things. Why would you expect different of him?" By saying that Scully was "impregnated with science," Carter is basically excusing this criminal act as a funny story they will tell their kids one day.

THE REVIVAL SEASONS

Seasons 10 and 11 are both extremely progressive and extremely regressive. The four "My Struggle" episodes, which bookend both seasons, were all written and directed by Chris Carter. They are a mess. All of them. For this essay, I will ignore the uneven pacing, the abandoned story threads, and the attempt to make the final "My Struggle" an action movie, and focus on the gender issues—of which there are several.

"My Struggle II," the Season 10 finale, was largely Scully's story. Mulder, weakened by the Spartanvirus, goes looking for the truth while Scully stays in the city, working up a cure for the virus that has been unleashed amongst the people. She is a total bad-ass, working to convince agents and nurses the conspiracy blather that would normally be coming from Mulder is true. In "My Struggle III," we discover that all of the previous episode was Scully's fever-dream, a vision sent to her by William, warning her of how the world will end. None of it happened. Instead, "My Struggle III" sees Scully mostly hospitalized, including a scene where she is nearly smothered to death, only to be saved at the last minute by Mulder with a scalpel. She's a bad-ass in her dream, but when it comes to "real life," she is a damsel in distress. She was never a damsel in distress before; why start now?

"My Struggle IV" had a similar problem. Mulder goes out playing Jason Bourne and killing a lot of bad guys while hunting down their son, but Scully sits at home and worries. My headcanon tells me that Scully found out she was pregnant at the top of the episode, and since she would be a high-risk pregnancy (she was fifty-four years old in the show), she decided not to risk her fetus by joining Mulder on his adventure up and down the Eastern Seaboard. That doesn't make it better, but it helps me sleep at night. And frankly, after Scully's continued trouble with fertility and babies, I cannot blame her for wanting to be more careful. But it would have been easy to give the audience a hint at her pregnancy without revealing it to Mulder until the final scene.

It is in this series finale that Scully finally finds out the truth about William's "parentage." The audience never gets to see her reaction to the news, which is another example of Scully getting robbed of the chance to deal with her reproductive autonomy (I address this more later on). This, and Scully being sidelined throughout the episode, deprives her of her voice, something which I always felt was strong and vibrant throughout the series. Would it have really killed Chris Carter to take two minutes from his excessive car chase scenes to give Scully some sort of closure?

Annabeth Gish feels the same way. The actress who played Monica Reyes starting in Season 8 told me that, rather than pointedly not giving Scully or Reyes closure, she thinks there simply wasn't enough time. "Oddly enough, there was a misstep in that they could have had that moment, a couple scenes between Scully and Reyes, and capitalized on the change that is happening for women in the industry. Gillian and I, of course, would have been on board," she explains. "Chris and Frank and the writers… no one is a misogynist. I only and always felt they were intelligent, respectful men. There is a part of the language and the conditioning and socialization that is just imprinted on all of us, and that is changing. I think it is good to go back and analyze, but not incriminate all the time. I don't think there was intentional misogyny at play. To go back and be punitive about it is not productive, nor is it fair to these creators."

Despite all of this, Season 11 was very progressive—just not in the "My Struggle" episodes. Mulder grows up over the course of Season 11. No longer is he this sad puppy dog chasing monsters. He is now chasing the love of his life, trying to win her back—while also chasing monsters. Scully's sexuality is also dealt with in a positive light in this season.

"Plus One" involves a case about evil doppelgangers that disturbs both agents and sends Scully to Mulder's bed. At first it is just to talk, but then *she* makes the decision to roll over and give him a sly look. At the episode's end, Mulder suggests they hit the hay before checkout. He insists he just means sleep, but Scully doubts his intentions and dismisses him from the room. That only lasts a few moments before *she* makes the decision to go find Mulder and take him up on his unspoken offer. In both instances, it is Scully making the overtures, and Scully going to him to get what *she* wants. Interestingly, this episode was written by Chris Carter, which shows that at some point over the course of the series, he became comfortable enough with female sexuality that he was able to let his female lead have sex—and at her discretion.

The most overt ode to Scully's sexuality comes in "Rm9sbG93ZXJz," an episode written by two women (Shannon Hamblin and Kristen Cloke Morgan). It is almost completely devoid of dialogue and had nothing to do with an X-File. Mulder and Scully go on a dinner date to an automated sushi restaurant. Mulder refuses to tip the robots, the robots get mad, and send legions of digital devices after them. After the date, Scully goes home and spills something. A drone delivers a Roomba-type vacuum immediately, which Scully puts to use. As it vacuums her home, it finds a small pink vibrator under her bed. Scully is not embarrassed; she almost seems pleased that the vacuum found it. She puts it in her pocket. Later, when she and Mulder realize the robots are tracking them based on their digital devices, they dump everything into a garbage can—including Scully's vibrator. Mulder looks surprised or maybe jealous, but Scully is still not embarrassed. She shrugs, as if to say, "A girl's gotta take care of herself."

CHRIS CARTER, SEXUALITY, AND ISSUES OF CONSENT

Unfortunately, "My Struggle III" was not the only example of rape being treated marginally in *The X-Files*. One of the most lauded episodes, Season 5's "The Post-Modern Prometheus," written and directed by Carter, is shot in black and white and framed like a comic book tale. In it, Mulder and Scully go to the middle of nowhere to investigate a mysterious, unexplainable pregnancy. It is a beautiful, quirky episode, well shot and well written—for the most part. The "big bad" in the episode is a horribly disfigured young man who has been kept in a barn away from people his whole life. At night, he breaks into houses with his father and dances to Cher while his father drugs and "impregnates with science" women. The idea is that another person who is equally disfigured would never leave the young man—your typical Bride of Frankenstein scenario.

In the end, the young man admits what he did was wrong, and the women are happy with their disfigured babies and their violation because it gets them onto *The Jerry Springer Show*. Unfortunately, because of his disfigurement and his lack of socialization, the agents take pity on him (more specifically, *Mulder* takes pity on him). Instead of taking him to jail, they take him to a Cher concert. Even if he eventually goes to prison, he is *rewarded* for his crimes. I know, I know—the young man did not physically touch these women, but I can't help but feel like if his father had been murdering these women, he would have been granted no clemency. (I should note that there are some theories that say this ending was in Mulder's head; his way of giving the story a better ending. There is nothing to confirm or deny this theory.)

Sexuality—especially female sexuality—seems to make Carter uncomfortable. This can be seen in the way he treats rape in "My Struggle III" and "The Post-Modern Prometheus." Some critics would also include Season 4's "Small Potatoes" in this category. In the episode, a shape shifter takes advantage of women by posing as their husbands and having sex with them. The humorous tone of the episode upsets many people, like it is making light of rape. I never found this to be an issue. The humor surrounds the character, not the act. The rapist *does* go to prison, and Carter did not write this episode.

Consensual sex seems to be ignored in *The X-Files*, too. Fans have taken issue with the fact that Scully has no romantic life until she finally sleeps with Mulder in Season 7. Again, fans and critics alike have forgotten the fact that Mulder did not have a sex life, either. There is heated debate within the fandom about whether or not Scully had sex with a man with a haunted tattoo in Season 4's "Never Again;" and whether or not Mulder had sex with a "vampire" in Season 2's "3." Regardless of your thoughts on this, the fact remains that neither of them ever had a significant other during the run of the show. They each had visits from past lovers, and Scully had one boring date in Season 1.

Perhaps Carter leaned too hard in the opposite direction of the "typical female lead." In the 1993-1994 TV season, when *The X-Files* premiered, there wasn't much in the way of female-driven TV shows. Of the top twenty shows, the closest thing to a Dana Scully that television had was *Murphy Brown,* a sitcom about a female journalist who was always more concerned with getting the story than getting the guy. There was also *Murder, She Wrote,* led by a post-menopausal woman who would not be thought of as a sexual being, and *Roseanne* and *Grace Under Fire,* both sitcoms in which the female leads were solely focused on domestic issues.

Carter *didn't* want his show to become a soap opera; nor did he want to water down the science-fiction, the monsters, the horror. This is why Mulder and Scully were "strictly platonic" for so many seasons. This worked for the show. It cracked the top twenty in its fourth season, and created a renaissance for genre television. Twenty-five years after the show premiered, it still has an extremely active fandom that debates the tiniest nuances of the show, the plot, and the characters.

Reproductive autonomy

Scully's reproductive autonomy has long been a hot topic amongst critics who say that Scully was treated horribly. Her continued trouble with her fertility was born out of real-life need for it (Gillian Anderson's pregnancy) and yes, it focused on Scully's procreative abilities more than it would for a man. Let's face it: women bear children. Men do not. It's as simple as that. Mulder's fertility could have been affected by various experiments and tortures he was subjected to over the series, but he wasn't having sex, and male infertility does not lead to a host of other health problems like female infertility can. If he was infertile, how would he even know?

Before Season 2 began filming, actress Gillian Anderson and her then-husband, *The X-Files* art director Clyde Klotz, found themselves unexpectedly pregnant. In order to allow Anderson time off to have the baby, Scully was abducted, presumably by aliens (though as we later find out, it was the government using alien technology). It seemed a perfect way to write Scully out of a couple episodes, especially in a show *about* aliens. It also brings the story around to Mulder's sister's abduction, a formative experience for him, and something that only brings him closer to Scully.

Scully's abduction became a major plot throughout the run of the entire series. Never has an actress's real-life pregnancy plot yielded so many consequences for a TV show. Because of her abduction, Scully's ova were stolen, leaving her infertile. She was also given cancer, and one of her ovum was used to create a hybrid child who Scully found out about just in time to watch die.

Ultimately, the whole story of that child, Emily, was pointless. The Emily plot was dealt with over the course of two Season 5 episodes ("Christmas Carol" and "Emily"), mentioned once a few episodes later, in an episode exploring Scully's faith ("All Souls") and never mentioned again. There are, however, remarkable similarities between Mulder's attempts to soothe Scully about Emily's fate, and Scully's attempts to soothe Mulder after learning the "truth" of William's parentage. Whether or not this was intentional on Carter's part is anyone's guess.

When Scully finds out she is pregnant in the Season 7 finale, this leads to a host of other problems with Scully's representation: she is supposedly infertile, yet here she is with a "miracle" baby; Mulder is abducted before she has a chance to tell him about the baby; and pregnant Scully becomes somehow "lesser." In the penultimate Season 8 episode, "Essence," there is a scene where a very pregnant Scully sits on a couch, while a group of men—Mulder, Doggett, Skinner, and Krycek—stand in a tight circle, talking *about* Scully and how to protect her, rather than talking *to* her or *with* her. I find this scene especially upsetting because it takes the strong, independent character I fell in love with, and turns her into the antithesis of who her character once was. This scene is more offensive to me than any other mistreatment of Scully throughout the series.

MULDER VS. SCULLY?

Some may say that the Emily storyline was just another way for Chris Carter to torture his female lead. And yes, Scully has been tortured plenty in this show: she has been kidnapped no fewer than five times, abducted by "aliens," was shot once (not including bullet grazes), given cancer, had her fertility stolen from her and still had a baby created from one of her ovum. What people seem to forget is that Mulder has faced just as much crap as Scully has: he has been kidnapped and/or beaten near death no fewer than five times, he was shot twice (not including bullet grazes), had a deadly brain disease, he gets abducted by *real* aliens and tortured in what the fandom calls the Dental Chair of Death, and he gets infected by the black oil. I would say that the mistreatment is pretty evenly divided. Mulder's own suffering should not be overlooked. Gender equality means equality on *all* fronts. A man's suffering should be considered as valid (or as horrible) as a woman's suffering.

In an extremely informal survey of fifty random episodes, I found that Mulder was victimized thirteen times, and Scully was victimized fifteen times. However, in nearly half those instances, Scully saved herself, and in nearly all of Mulder's instances, Scully saved him.

For example, in Season 4's "Leonard Betts," Betts accosts Scully, but she beats the hell out of him and defibrillates his head, killing him. In Season 6's "Triangle," Mulder travels back in time when he goes looking for a cruise ship that disappeared in the Bermuda Triangle. While he makes it back to the present on his own, it was only because of Scully's frantic efforts that Mulder was rescued from the icy water before he could die.

Each time that Mulder saves Scully, it is with a traditional show of brute force: Mulder slits the throat of a man trying to smother Scully (Season 11's "My Struggle III"); he shoots a man about to behead her for a cannibalistic ritual (Season 2's "Our Town"); he kills an author obsessed with Scully who has sent his "imaginary friend" to kill her (Season 6's "Milagro"). But when Scully saves Mulder, it is with a show of fierce determination, take-no-shit attitude, and deep scientific understanding. It is Scully's scientific documentation that saves Mulder's life after the pair are trapped on an abandoned ship with a water supply that causes accelerated aging (Season 2's "Dod Kalm"). It is Scully who insists that field doctors keep Mulder in an icy tub, knowing that the freezing temperature is the only thing keeping a mysterious virus from killing him (Season 2's "Colony" & "End Game"). It is Scully who figures out while performing an autopsy that the drug is in the pizza she left Mulder eating (Season 5's "Bad Blood"). But Scully *does* get to go bad-ass when she enters a virtual reality video game with a big machine gun to rescue Mulder (Season 7's "First Person Shooter").

In Season 5, "Kill Switch" sees Mulder and Scully caught up in a world of artificial intelligence and virtual reality. Mulder gets sucked into a simulation when the computer wants to get the "kill switch" from him in order to save itself. The computer uses a combination of ultra-sexy vixen nurses to get him to spill, and when that doesn't work, the nurses threaten him. That doesn't work either, so the computer sends in Scully to kick the nurses' asses and save Mulder. His excitement isn't just over being saved; it is about *Scully* saving him. What's more is that she is in her traditional pantsuit and sensible pumps.

Danielle at The Radical Notion[3] sees the show as pitting Mulder and Scully against each other. She admits that Scully is a feminist icon, but still takes issue with the show itself. In her essay, "The Feminism of *The X-Files*," Danielle states: "For example, Mulder was and is very much the decision-maker despite their partnership, most often insisting that he is right and Scully is wrong.... He mansplains to her and is dismissive of her spiritual beliefs and opinions." The X-Files was Mulder's department; Mulder's baby. Scully was assigned to, essentially, babysit him. Of course he will be making the decisions. And Scully insists that she is right, and Mulder is wrong just as frequently. He may be dismissive of her religion, but she is equally dismissive of his belief in aliens and conspiracies.

Danielle also uses the following line as proof of the gender imbalance: "I mean, at one point he even tells her that he insists on driving because he's not sure that 'her little feet would reach the pedals.' That, to me, does not an equal partnership make." That line comes from the Season 3 episode "Syzygy," in which an astrological alignment makes everyone in town act erratically, irrationally, and snarkily. Both Mulder and Scully were at each other's throats the entire episode—until midnight, when the alignment shifted, and everyone returned to normal. Taken out of context, of course it sounds bad. But within the context of that particular episode, it is purely an example of how severe the astrological convergence is.

Ira Madison III has a similar complaint about the Season 10 episode, "Mulder and Scully Meet the Were-Monster." As Madison states in an article for The Daily Beast[4] about the show's reboot, "Even the reboot's best episode goes to almost comical lengths to make Scully a pratfalling secondary character in the episode so Mulder can save the day." The title alone should prove that the episode was *supposed* to be comical: it is a direct reference to the Abbott and Costello films of the 1940s and 1950s, in which the comedy duo meet Frankenstein, the Mummy, and the Invisible Man. I assume that the scene Madison is referring to, in which Scully is a "pratfalling secondary character," is the Were-Monster bragging about his sexual prowess with Scully, which has her playing the comical bimbo and having sex with him in the back room. But that scene was all part of the Were-Monster's vivid imagination. Mulder has his own "pratfalling" moments too, namely as he tries—and fails—to figure out how to use the camera on his phone. Most importantly, Mulder *doesn't* save the day. It

---

3. http://www.theradicalnotion.com/feminism-of-the-x-files/

4. https://www.thedailybeast.com/the-x-files-returns-and-continues-to-disrespect-scully

is Scully who figures out who the killer is, and it is Scully who arrests him. By the time Mulder shows up, the killer is being dragged away in cuffs. There is nothing left for Mulder to do. Scully does not have nearly as much screen time as Mulder does in this episode; perhaps that is why Madison sees Scully as a secondary character? If so, that is an extremely limited way to view the show.

THE SCULLY EFFECT

Though it has only become an accepted mainstream theory recently, I remember hearing about The Scully Effect back in the late 1990s. This is the idea that the character Dana Scully was solely responsible for a marked increase in the rate of women going into the traditionally male-dominated fields of science, medicine, and law enforcement.

In 2018, the Geena Davis Institute on Gender in Media[5] conducted the first research study to evidentially confirm what had previously only been anecdotal. In a survey of 2,021 female participants, aged 25 and older, 63 percent of the respondents said that Dana Scully "increased their belief in the importance of STEM" and "increased their confidence that they could excel in a male-dominated profession." Among women in STEM careers, that same percentage say that Scully served as their role model. A whopping 91 percent of all respondents said that Scully was a role model for girls and women.

The influence of Dana Scully on young women cannot be understated. Anne Simon is a virologist and professor who acted as the science advisor on *The X-Files* over the show's eleven seasons. In an interview with Vice[6], Simon shares an anecdote about her Intro Biology class. When asked who was inspired by Dana Scully to go into science fields, half the hands in class went up. "Kids were given a real positive science role model [in Scully]. She was smart; she didn't know everything about everything, [but] she consulted with people. She was helpful, she was skeptical—but she was open-minded, especially as time went on. She wasn't closed off and she had a great relationship with Mulder, and I think people could see themselves."

---

5. https://impact.21cf.com/wp-content/uploads/sites/2/2018/03/ScullyEffectReport_21CF_1-1.pdf

6. https://motherboard.vice.com/en_us/article/nzeppk/the-new-x-files-science-advisor-explains-how-the-reboot-will-stay-realistic

Chris Carter fought the network to prevent Scully from being turned into a leggy, vacuous blonde, there only to be ogled by male viewers. In doing so, he created one of the most iconic characters in television history. There may have been missteps along the way, but this cannot and should not be forgotten. Despite the sensitivity the era of #metoo has brought, this should not mean we have to go back and retcon the importance of Dana Scully.

Elvira, Mistress of My Heart

by Heidi Honeycutt

IT WAS A DARK AND STORMY NIGHT. Not really. It was *almost* dark, but pretty much just California sunset. Back before global warming, when Los Angeles wasn't the hellish fiery desert it is today, there was sometimes fog in the hills of the Santa Monica Mountains. This fog would swirl around the house I grew up in as the sun went down during autumn evenings. My sister and I would lie on the brown carpet of our living room, in front of the old TV that had no remote and only eight channels (my parents had the same TV from 1966 through 1989 and refused to get cable or modernize in any way). We would manually dial the TV to Channel 9. That's when the magic would happen.

The living room would transform into a terrifying haunted house. Simple, but eerie, electronic organ music would abruptly begin playing as the TV screen dimmed and blurred. A tall, beautiful woman dressed in a revealing black evening gown would open a creaky door and sensually walk down a misty hallway as thunder and lightning cut across the screen. The words "Movie Macabre" with "Elvira, Mistress of the Dark" were superimposed across this tableau, which would then fade out to a set piece composed of only an elaborate red velvet sofa and a set of two old-fashioned candelabras with lit white candles. The background was usually dark so it was just Elvira, her couch, the candles, and sometimes a telephone that signaled the start of my favorite television show: *Movie Macabre*.

I can't remember the name of three different guys I made out with in high school. I can't remember my address from ten years ago. I sure as hell can't remember much of anything after getting rear-ended and suffering a concussion in December 2017, but I will always remember this aforementioned *Movie Macabre* scene vividly because of how deeply it struck me to the very core. Elvira was awesome. Sure, I was like three years old at the time, and my life experience consisted of cartoons and Tinker Toys, but even then I knew: I wanted to be just like her.

Up until age ten, the only female pop culture icons I understood besides Elvira were Marilyn Monroe, Madonna, and Lucille Ball. Maybe Ginger from *Gilligan's Island*. There was one thing I knew: women can be funny, or they can be pretty. But they can't be both. I couldn't fit Elvira into this equation at all, because Elvira was both. My mind exploded. Elvira exploded my brain. I wanted to be pretty and funny together at the same time.

Marilyn Monroe was just as sexy as Elvira, and arguably one of the most beautiful women to have ever lived. Even if Andy Warhol had not immortalized the cruelty and commoditization of celebrity with his Marilyn Monroe series in the 1960s, Monroe would still have been one of the most recognizable pop culture icons of the twentieth century, right along with Elvis Presley. We remember Monroe for her beauty, her incomparable charm, and her disturbingly sexy innocence. She embodied these exquisitely passionate enchantments in some of her most famous performances: as the troubled babysitter Nell Forbes in *Don't Bother to Knock* (1952); as the abused but adorable Cherie in *Bus Stop* (1956), and the stunningly untrustworthy Rose Loomis in *Niagara* (1953). But anyone who has seen *Some like It Hot* (1959), *Gentlemen Prefer Blondes* (1953), *How to Marry a Millionaire* (1953), *The Prince and the Showgirl* (1957), *Monkey Business* (1952), or *The Seven Year Itch* (1955) knows that Monroe was a very talented comedian with impeccable timing and a knack for physical gags. She knew how to play up her own sex appeal as part of the punch line. Why is she not remembered for these hilarious performances that surely outnumber her photo shoots and birthday songs? Because being remembered as funny would make her memory less attractive to our strange, sexist culture. Western culture likes hot women, and they like funny women, but not when they are mashed together.

Lucille Ball was sexy. Have you ever seen the 1946 noir *The Dark Corner* in which a stunning Ball tells the leading man Clifton Webb that everything went "Busto Crusto?" In startling contrast, Lucy Ricardo, her character from the 1950s TV series *I Love Lucy*, is an awkward, bumbling, and inevitably thwarted person who only happens to also look good when she cleans up. Lucille Ball is remembered as Lucy Ricardo, and the funny, gorgeous woman gets buried in the stereotypes molded by twentieth century media.

Cassandra Peterson is funny. Therefore, Elvira is funny. Cassandra Peterson is also beautiful. Head exploding. She's also a horror icon. Head is mush.

Before she was Elvira, Peterson was a dancer in Las Vegas, and had sex with Elvis Presley (according to rumors). She had a few minor roles such as "Stripper" in a few major films and posed semi-nude for the cover of Tom Waits' album *Small Change*—though she claims to have no recollection of posing for it. She spent most of the 1970s touring nightclubs in the United States and in Italy, singing in rock bands and performing in musical/comedy acts.

When Peterson auditioned for the role of horror hostess for a new TV series, she incorporated a few brilliant ideas that would shape the vision of women in comedy and women in horror for… well, for eternity. In addition to the black dress, black wig, pale skin, and sexy horror personality that the producers had wanted originally, Peterson added her own twist: Elvira was a sarcastic, quick-witted Valley Girl, taking down the bad horror movies she showed with clever quips.

Before casting Peterson as Elvira, the producers of the show had sought to recast the aging Maila Nurmi and use the character she had created in the 1950s: the original black-clad sexpot TV horror hostess Vampira. When producers wouldn't cast Lola Falana as Vampira, Nurmi took her character and left. Nurmi later filed a lawsuit against Cassandra Peterson (*Nurmi v. Peterson, 1989)*, claiming that Elvira was a rip-off of Vampira. Nurmi wanted a piece of the sweet, sweet merchandising money that came from using Elvira's likeness to sell products and promote events. Weighing the black dress, the hair, the similar mannerisms, the horror hosting, and a myriad of other factors, the court decided that Peterson had not done anything illegal by creating a similar character:

> The plaintiff does not allege that the defendants created Elvira to look exactly like Vampira but rather asserts that defendants used some of the plaintiff's props, clothes, and mannerisms. Given these allegations, the Court finds that the defendants did not appropriate the plaintiff's name, voice, signature, photograph, or likeness. Thus, the plaintiff's second claim under §3344 is dismissed.[1]

---

1. District Court, C.D. California. *Nurmi v. Peterson.* No. CV 88-5436-WMB. Decided March 31, 1989

What may have contributed most to this court decision was that Nurmi's Vampira was, herself, a rip-off of *The Addams Family* ghoulish-but-lovely character Morticia Addams.

Peterson further developed the character of Elvira with the show's producers, trying a few different angles, eventually settling on the slightly punk, Valley Girl version of Elvira. The jokes were abundant. The character was brilliant and resonated with horror fans everywhere. Elvira was not like most women in horror films: continuously stalked and murdered by maniacs and perverts, eternally the victims. She was in control of the horror and in control of the perverts. When the recurring character The Breather (played by John Paragon) would call Elvira on the telephone during her intros and joke segments, instead of the intimidating, dirty talk one would expect from a creep, he'd just tell her weird jokes, and she'd disgustedly hang up the phone without an ounce of terror. She was the monster. She had nothing to fear. She made fun of the movies and the other monsters, not the other way around. And she was hilarious.

Elvira is not a rip-off of Maila Nurmi's Vampira, but I have to say, there's an ungodly amount of Mae West hanging out in the character. Elvira spouted numerous one-liners, often sexual, on almost every episode of *Movie Macabre*. Just a few of her better ones include: "I'm glad to see you're back. You're glad to see my front;" "The show, as you know, is *Movie Macabre*. And week after week that's exactly what we show...Week. No... I mean Macabre!" and, "If this makes anyone in the audience feel sick, put your head between your knees and enjoy yourselves." In a scene in the feature film *Elvira, Mistress of the Dark* (1988), a bartender tells her that there's no hard liquor served after eight o'clock. "Do you want a virgin?" he asks her. She responds with "Maybe, but, ah... I'll have a couple of drinks first."

Mae West was a tremendously talented comedian and actress from the 1930s most noted for her incredibly curvy figure and outrageous sex jokes. She wrote the majority of her own lines and gags and was a fan of crass but poetic euphemisms and puns. She was notorious for being blatantly sexual and portraying characters that suffered no consequences for their blatant promiscuity. Her sense of humor was unlike anything anyone had seen a woman do in comedy up until that time. "When I'm good, I'm very good. But when I'm bad, I'm better," she wisecracks in *I'm No Angel* (1933). Pop culture has pinned the quote "Come up and see me sometime" on West, also from the same movie, much in the way that most horror fans remember Elvira's catchphrase at the end of every episode: "Unpleasant dreams..."

The character of Elvira never faced any censorship, but in her film *Elvira, Mistress of the Dark*, Elvira faces censorship and accusations of corrupting the youth by the local townspeople she meets. The uptight, religious Chastity Pariah (played brilliantly by character actress Edie McClurg) calls for Elvira to be burned as a witch, referring to her as "morally unfit" and that "Elvira is person of easy virtue, a purveyor of pulchritude, a one-woman Sodom and Gomorrah, if you will. A slimy, slithering succubus, a concubine, a street walker, a tramp, a slut, a cheap whore." Perhaps channeling Mae West's actual persecution in Hollywood, Elvira is an example of a woman that threatens our culture's idea of womanhood, and she suffers the same kind of accusations. Elvira actually is a witch in *Elvira, Mistress of the Dark* so perhaps we shouldn't be so hard on Chastity.

Elvira did something very strange that launched me into a lifetime of love for horror films as well as created an inordinate interest in the way women fit into the genre: she made me less afraid of horror. When the horror host is on your side and has an undeniable handle on the horror films she's showing, you feel safer. The horrible things you see on-screen are torn apart during the commercial segues and they become jokes. Horror, even the most sincerely serious of horror, is not safe from a character like Elvira. I believe this is where my obsession with horror films really developed: I could be a woman, like Elvira, and I could be "in control" of the horror and not the other way around. I could write the stories, or write about the stories, or watch the films being made, or analyze the villains and subvert the monsters, make the grotesque and lowly the subjects of intense intellectual study or of even cruder jokes. I could take their power away, thereby becoming more powerful in my own right and an arbiter of my own destiny in a sense. I could be in charge of what scares me, not the other way around. I could even be hilarious and funny, and if Chastity Pariah came to get me, I could tell her to fuck off and mean it. Elvira created a whole new type of person that I could look up to: a funny, sexy woman who loves horror.

In 2019, there are numerous hilarious, gorgeous women that love horror. Because of my strange life enmeshed in this "horror community" I probably know them all. They're amazing. We support one another and we celebrate our shared hobby of horror films. The men seem pretty supportive of us, too. It's almost as if we're all allowed to just be the people we want to be, instead of having to try to fit into what a woman or a man is supposed to be: a victim or a killer or something else entirely. We're pretty free to express ourselves in this subculture in a way humans in the Western world have not been able to for many centuries.

I think we all love Elvira. I am not sure if we are all fascinated by her sexuality the way I am, or if anyone else is actively seeking out Mae West references in any of her joke material, but everyone who loves horror recognizes that Elvira is entertaining, endearing, and makes us feel good.

I have to credit some of my more obscure and demented horror interests to Elvira's *Movie Macabre*. It's that "dark and stormy night" and I'm not even five years old, but I'm glued to the television waiting for the show to start. I saw films for which I had no cultural context and no adult to guide me, other than Elvira herself: *The Devil's Rain* (1975), *The Incredible Melting Man* (1977), *The Devil's Wedding Night* (1973), *The Legend of Hell House* (1973), *House of Dark Shadows* (1970), and dozens more.

I had a vision of a beautiful Italian woman wearing a glowing red ring stuck in my head for *years* until I realized it was from a scene in *The Devil's Wedding Night* that had aired on *Movie Macabre*. I still have horrific dreams about rattlesnakes covering the floor and cornering me; these nightmares are because *Rattlers* (1976) made a distinct impression on me when it aired on *Movie Macabre*. Another image, of body parts and torsos strewn in the trees of a foreboding forest, has haunted me life-long; I was able to discover that this is a memory of the 1967 horror film *The Torture Chamber of Dr. Sadism*, which I saw on *Movie Macabre* as a child. It was only last night that another creepy, demented, horrific memory that has been in my brain since the age of four was at long last revealed to be the ending of *The Beast in the Cellar* (1971) which, again, aired on *Movie Macabre*.

The only other horror memory I have that intensely that did not come from watching *Movie Macabre* is the *Hammer House of Horror* TV episode "Children of the Moon," a moment when a woodcutter transforms into a werewolf. After that, the memories are clear, but they don't haunt or disturb me the way *Movie Macabre* does. *The Howling* (1981) certainly created some night terrors (a werewolf was planning on jumping through the glass of my bedroom window to eat me, I just knew it) and one time on regular weekend daytime TV, the network airing *The Shining* (1980) forgot to edit out the nude lady corpse scene (that kind of thing used to happen all the time back then, the golden age of lackadaisical TV movie censorship), but my formative, impressionable mind had already been molded by the haunted castles, misty mountains, vampiric nightmares, and hilarious sex banter of Elvira's *Movie Macabre*.

I had the extremely good fortune of meeting and interviewing Elvira in 2007 at an open casting call for a Fox TV series called *The Search for the Next Elvira*. I was hosting a horror TV series pilot for the now-extinct Scream TV channel, and I went to cover the casting call aboard the Queen Mary in Long Beach, California. I held a microphone and interviewed a lot of the gals auditioning; many of them were amazingly well put together with gorgeous, elaborate hair and makeup, giant breasts, props, and a fantastic attitude. I was a skinny redhead in a pink skirt. I did not, in any way, look as though I could ever be Elvira, or anything like her. But man, I auditioned anyway. I asked Elvira what I could do about my boobs and she did tell me that yeah, I could use a little padding, but we could make it work. She was very charming, and nice to me.

The best thing that happened during that interview was that I got to watch a few other people audition for the spot. Those auditioning had to read the introduction for the new version of *Movie Macabre*, which sounds simple enough. Peterson, in character as Elvira, had to immediately cut short one woman's audition and kick her out because she had pronounced *Movie Macabre* as *Movie Makah-bree*.

The world never got to see my interview with Elvira on an actual TV channel, but it's floating around on YouTube, and I enjoy looking at it from time to time because it proves to me, and to the world, that I did meet my hero, Elvira, Mistress of the Dark. I am pretty sure Cassandra Peterson is actually also my hero; you have to be pretty funny and clever to come up with a character that good and to stick with it and to have a line around the block for your autograph. Peterson saw the best in Vampira, Mae West, Morticia Addams, and bad horror films, which automatically makes her one of the best people to ever exist. I love her. She'll never remember me, but I will always remember her.

Unpleasant Dreams.

Passing Into Myth: *Candyman* and the Final Woman

by Stacie Ponder

"In the end, we'll all become stories. Or else we'll become entities. Maybe it's the same."

– Margaret Atwood

I SAW *CANDYMAN* DURING its original theatrical run, and I tell ya, I damn near lost my mind. It was 1992, and it wasn't exactly a Golden Age for horror. We were inundated with goofiness, whether it was sequels in franchises that were well-past their sell-by date or dopey flicks that had nothing vital to say and wouldn't scare a toddler.

But *Candyman* was different. After we left the theater, my friends and I went straight to the nearest cemetery where we would test our courage by attempting to summon the film's hook-handed villain. Sure, according to the legend put forth in the movie, it's looking into a mirror as you say "Candyman" five times that'll cause him to appear behind you. But wouldn't our odds be increased if we tried it in a cemetery in the dark of night? Ah, the indisputable logic of youth hopped up on candy, soda, and a horror movie.

We parked in a remote corner of the graveyard, got out of the car, and began. "Candyman, Candyman, Candyman…"

No one would say his name more than three times before going silent or ending up in a fit of nervous giggles. It's not that we really believed he'd show up—we weren't *that* young. But everyone who summoned him in the film ended up dead in a large pool of blood, gutted like a fish. Was that a chance we really wanted to take? We went home, calling the whole idea "stupid," which it surely was. But mostly we were just scared.

In the *oh God, how many years has it been* since then, Candyman has, like Jason Voorhees, Freddy Krueger, and Michael Myers before him, become a bona fide horror icon. What sets the film apart from the vast majority of its slasher brethren, however, is how damn smart it is and how many layers it has. *Candyman* addresses sexism, issues of class and poverty, America's history of racism and the repercussions, as well as the power of myth and oral histories. It was groundbreaking on release in its blatant exploration of these themes and it still feels transgressive and important today, and perhaps more relevant than ever. It's also as terrifying as ever.

While researching urban legends for their joint thesis, grad students Helen Lyle (Virginia Madsen) and Bernadette Walsh (Kasi Lemmons) repeatedly hear the tale of Candyman, as recounted by freshman interviewees. Everyone knows someone who knows someone who told someone about someone who died by his hook hand, or survived the encounter but went insane, or disappeared altogether. It's kid's stuff, akin to swearing that Bloody Mary killed your cousin's girlfriend's cousin *for real* or that last year a girl in your dorm went mad after she woke up one morning and saw "Aren't you glad you didn't turn on the light?" written on the wall in blood.

Henrietta, one of the university's cleaning women, overhears the Candyman story as Helen transcribes an interview and promptly grounds him in reality. "Everybody's scared of him once it gets dark," she says. "He lives over in Cabrini. My friend told me about him." Unlike the students with their tall tales, Henrietta can even produce another cleaning woman, Kitty, who backs up Henrietta's claims and elaborates: a young woman named Ruthie Jean called 911 several times when she heard someone coming through the wall of her apartment in the Cabrini-Green housing projects. No one came to her aid, and she died after Candyman split her open with his hook. Neither Kitty nor Henrietta would go on record, lest Candyman do the same to them in retaliation.

Helen investigates as any good cinematic heroine from a certain era must: by taking to the microfiche machine. She finds the sad story of Ruthie Jean, who was, in fact, murdered after no one answered her cries for help. But Candyman couldn't really be responsible… could he? During her research, Helen makes another startling discovery: her fancy apartment building is actually nothing more than a housing project with a fresh coat of paint and some sprucing up. While Cabrini-Green had train tracks and freeways separating it from the high-priced Gold Coast neighborhood, Helen's building had no such buffer zone. Developers covered the cinder block walls in plaster, put in fancy windows, gave each unit an exorbitant price tag, and sold them off as condos. Some tricks of cheap construction remain, however: Helen is able to remove her medicine cabinet and push through to the empty neighboring apartment. She surmises that Ruthie Jean's killer was able to enter her apartment the same way—he did, in fact, come right through her wall.

In 1992, Chicago's real-life Cabrini-Green housing project was fifty years old and seen by the masses as a cautionary tale about public housing. Decades of neglect left the buildings run-down, with boarded-up windows, overflowing garbage, all manner of vermin infestation, and burnt-out, empty apartments. Individual buildings were controlled by various gangs who covered hallways, stairwells, doors, and windows and kept tenants living in fear. Murder and violence were commonplace. Fenced-in balconies and cement yards were intended to save both tenant lives and landscaping costs, but ultimately they made the area look like an elaborate wasteland prison system. Cabrini-Green was notorious in the eyes of the public, the embodiment of the terrifying "otherness" of the inner city.

During this time, the slasher subgenre was strictly the domain of the teenager, both onscreen and in the audience. Horny dumb-dumbs would shack up at an isolated location, get naked, and get killed in bloody fashion. Said horny dumb-dumbs were often completely inconsequential, often interchangeable, and frequently nameless save the Final Girl. The killer was the star of the show, and usually the one the audience rooted for. It's all the more surprising, then, that *Candyman* would address the moral and racial panic about the "urban plight" directly.

Helen decides to visit Ruthie Jean's apartment to see if her theory is correct. Bernadette reluctantly tags along, well aware of Cabrini-Green's reputation and the possible repercussions for two young women waltzing into what is essentially a war zone. She's armed with pepper spray, but Helen is convinced that their appearance alone will protect them, that they look enough like cops to get a pass from the gangbangers loitering outside. The situation is tense but they only suffer a bit of verbal harassment as they make their way upstairs. (It could have proved much worse: in 1970, gang members killed two police officers as they walked across the Cabrini-Green baseball field.) The contrast between Helen's naive attitude and Bernadette's caution and wariness are stark reminders of how the two move through the world as a white woman and a black woman respectively. One is afforded faith that "it'll all be fine" while the other must live her life on her guard, constantly aware of her surroundings.

And yet, once they're inside the apartment building, Bernadette herself is seen as "other." Helen and Bernadette introduce themselves to Ruthie Jean's neighbor Anne Marie with handshakes and kindness. "White folks that come around here ain't too hand-shakin' with us," she says, looking at both women. Helen doesn't acknowledge it, but Bernadette is clearly taken aback by how she is seen by another young black woman. While she is more aware of the realities than her colleague, Bernadette is still far removed from life in Cabrini-Green. The "whiteness" bestowed upon her by Anne Marie is a concept, more about class and privilege than about skin color. Bernadette is visibly shaken by this and shrinks back, lingers quietly apart from the other two women as they fawn over Anne Marie's infant son. It's a small moment, one that could easily be completely overlooked, but it's remarkably powerful.

Helen makes a solo return trip to the projects to talk and research further. She cajoles Jake, a frightened young boy, into telling her where Candyman is; he leads her to a public restroom outside the apartment building where Candyman mutilated a special needs child. Helen enters the filthy outbuilding alone, and almost immediately she comes face to face with the notorious killer. He does indeed wield a hook, but he's just a man. A vicious man, but a flesh and blood mortal all the same. Helen is severely beaten by this gang leader, but Jake calls for help. She's rescued and recovers, unlike Ruthie Jean.

Helen and the film itself directly address the reason for this. Ruthie Jean was just another black casualty of "life in the projects," whereas a white woman getting assaulted called for action. Ruthie Jean called for help several times, and her calls went unanswered. Little attempt was made to solve her murder, and she was forgotten by all except fearful neighbors who listened to her screams as she was killed. After Helen encountered "Candyman," however, the response was completely different: the building was put on lockdown and the gang leader was flushed out and arrested. Helen is thankful that he's off the streets, but the injustice of Ruthie Jean's death (and the way all the Cabrini inhabitants are treated like second-class citizens) help fuel her desire to publish her thesis and make the story public. It's a touch "white savior"-y, perhaps, but Helen Lyle's heart was in the right place.

The drug lord Candyman may have been vanquished, but he was only a regular man with a name stolen from a myth. We learn more about the legend of Candyman, and its basis in history from Purcell, the smarmy professor who is more than happy to school the two "beautiful" grad students who dare challenge him and his work with their efforts.

Candyman was born the son of a slave who invented a means for mass-producing shoes. He grew up in polite society and studied at the best schools, and he would go on to become a well-known portrait artist. He fell in love with (and impregnated) one of his subjects, the white daughter of a wealthy landowner. The landowner hired a mob to track Candyman down; they chased him to what would eventually be the site of Cabrini-Green, sawed off his right hand, shoved a hook into the bloody stump, smeared honey over him, and let the angry bees of a local apiary sting him to death. His body was burned on a pyre and his ashes spread over Cabrini-Green, which Purcell has informally dubbed "Candyman country."

This macabre history grew and changed over the years, becoming the urban legend the university students were familiar with. Locals attributed their daily troubles and strife to "Candyman," and both the myth and the man who stole his name fed on their fear. The drug lord used that to control the populace, and the mythical Candyman used it to live. The tenants whispering his name allowed him to exist and granted him a type of immortality: he was literally the product of their imagination. With his namesake off the streets, however, his name wasn't bandied about as much. His very existence was threatened when the gang leader—his namesake—wasn't around any longer to perpetuate the stories and the terror. And so Candyman—summoned by Helen when she says his name in a mirror five times—must "shed innocent blood."

During the film, Helen is framed for a series of murders by Candyman. Bernadette is slaughtered in Helen's apartment; Anne Marie returns home one day and finds her dog dead, her son missing, and Helen covered in blood, wielding a cleaver. Helen loses everything from the life she knew: her apartment, her best friend, and her philandering husband, Trevor. She is locked up in prison, accused of murder, declared mentally ill and remanded to a hospital, only to escape after Candyman kills her doctor. Helen is blamed for all of the bloodshed and death by the public, her friends and family, and, most importantly, by Candyman himself. Like so many men who blame women for the violent atrocities they commit, this mythical killer essentially says "Look what you made me do!" every time he guts someone with his hook.

Candyman is a classic example of toxic masculinity, abusing and gaslighting the woman he sees as his. "It was always you, Helen," he seductively tells her time and again as she spirals deeper into despair. Still, the film grants him pity for the suffering he, too, endured. Candyman's story and Helen's story intertwine with each other and mirror one another: both are examples of what happens when people only see and believe the worst in you. No one thinks Helen is innocent in all the murders, and black men (and women) are rarely afforded the benefit of the doubt in any circumstance.

Helen eventually kills Candyman, but she dies as a result of injuries sustained when rescuing Anne Marie's son from a raging bonfire in a lot by Cabrini-Green. This selfless act keeps her name on the lips of the locals, and thus Helen, like Candyman before her, passes into myth. She becomes a new kind of Final Girl—a Final Woman, if you will—one who does not merely survive an encounter with a mad killer. She transcends, takes up the mantel, and becomes a kind of avenging angel. The film ends as Helen returns, summoned when a regretful Trevor mutters her name five times in a mirror. She appears behind him, a beautiful and terrifying specter, and uses the hook granted to her by the denizens of Cabrini-Green to gut her cheating ex-husband.

This striking moment speaks to the enduring power of storytelling and oral histories. In death, Helen is finally granted the power she was denied by all the men in her life, whether they were corporeal or mythical. Even in its final moments, *Candyman* is a political film, one that holds a mirror up to us and forces us to confront society's ills.

It's also just, you know, one hell of an ending for a horror film that is nothing short of an intense, bloody rollercoaster ride throughout. Audiences are satisfied when the jerk in a horror movie meets a bad end, when the zombies tear apart the loudmouthed bully, or the racist unbeliever is murdered by ghosts. When Trevor finally gets his, it's pure catharsis. My friends and I cheered when we saw it in a theater all those years ago, and it's still whoop-worthy. I introduced a friend to the film recently (one of my goals is to introduce everyone I meet to this underrated gem) and they were brought to their feet, yelping with delight, by Helen's revenge. Say her name five times and let her live forever.

Trick 'R Treat

by Shannon McGrew

BACK IN 2009, there was one movie I was in search of, a movie that was surrounded by mystique and curiosities ever since it was announced it was going straight to DVD. The movie I'm talking about is Michael Dougherty's feature film release *Trick 'R Treat*, and I was on a hunt to find it.

It was the afternoon of October 6th, 2009, and the sun was high in the sky as I made my way to the video store to make the only purchase I knew I had to make. With the sale complete, and the movie in my possession, I raced home to watch what I had been waiting months for, having no knowledge of the profound effect that this film would eventually have on my life. If you are wondering why I searched for this film, the answer is simple: it was filled with controversy and people who had seen early screenings wouldn't stop talking about how fantastic it was.

The rumors that I initially heard centered around the film being shelved due to excessive violence towards children and that Warner Bros. didn't feel comfortable releasing the film theatrically. IMDb posted a multitude of reasons ranging from competition with another horror film coming out at the same time (*Saw IV* [2007]) to the box-office failure of *Superman Returns* (2006) which was co-written by Michael Dougherty. For whatever reason, there has never been a clear indicator as to why the film was shelved for so long, but it only fueled the fire within me to get my hands on a copy.

For those not familiar with *Trick 'R Treat*, it's a horror anthology that takes place on Halloween night, featuring five interlocking stories which include the secret life of a high-school principal; a teen prank that results in deadly consequences; a college virgin in search of the perfect partner; a couple who disrespects the traditions of Halloween; and a miserable old man who is visited by a terrifying trick-or-treater. The thread that ties these stories together is Sam, a child-like trick-or-treater decked out in a set of orange-colored pajamas and a burlap sack. Sam, otherwise known as Samhain, is the keeper of Halloween customs, making sure no one desecrates the rules that have been set forth, for if they do, he's the one who will reign havoc upon them.

For the past eleven years, *Trick 'R Treat* has been a source of entertainment and comfort for me, no matter when I watched it. As the years ticked by, I developed a preoccupation with the pivotal character, Sam. There's something about this creature that speaks to me, and it wasn't until recently that I came to understand what that was. Sam is a celebration of all that is weird, all that is dark, and all that is unspoken. He doesn't entertain bullying, disrespect or threats. Instead, he thrives on the mischief and mayhem that befalls Halloween and welcomes with open arms those of us who love the strange and unusual. You see, Sam accepts you for who you are, no matter how weird or eccentric you may be to the "normal" world, and that level of understanding and recognition is what ultimately drew me to this film.

If you were to ask me when my obsession with Sam truly started, I wouldn't be able to pinpoint it. What I do know is that this film has been a source of comfort for me during the hardest times of my life, whether that be when I was struggling with bouts of depression or crawling out of a hole of despair after tragedy struck. Regardless of the issue, I kept going back to this movie, and it wasn't until this year that I truly understood why. Sam made me feel safe, and still does, which would account for why I have such a large collection of memorabilia dedicated to him. Though I have pieces throughout my entire home, I've managed to build a shrine in my office devoted to all things Sam and *Trick 'R Treat*. This has grown to include dozens of Sam plush toys, artwork, custom pieces, and promotional items from the film's release. Situated in the middle of this vast collection are three versions of the movie—the DVD, a Blu-ray copy, and the recently released Shout! Factory Collector's Edition Blu-ray. Each of these versions holds a special place in my heart which is why I'll never part with them or any piece in my collection. Each tells a story, a reason behind why I got it, and I would never give that up for anything.

My love for this film doesn't stop at just Sam, but reaches past that to the man who created *Trick 'R Treat*, writer/director Michael Dougherty. Here's a man that took everything that I love about Halloween and made it into a perfectly executed film that showcases so much more than just a holiday. The film transports me back home to New England, growing up outside of Salem, MA, and trick-or-treating in the crisp fall air with multicolored leaves falling all around. Dougherty was able to capture a portion of my childhood in this film. Having devoured the book *Trick 'r Treat: Tales of Mayhem, Mystery, and Mischief*, I learned just how much Sam meant to Dougherty through a series of his illustrations which eventually became a short film titled "Season's Greetings." Sam has been a fixture in Dougherty's life long before the inception of *Trick 'R Treat*, which goes to show how important this character is to him.

I had the chance to meet Dougherty at a pre-screening of his other holiday film, *Krampus* (2015), and I have never been so nervous in my life. As I practiced my lines in my head, I nervously approached him with my DVD copy of *Trick 'R Treat* and my poster. With shaking hands, I asked if he would sign both while mumbling about the importance of his film to me. He graciously accepted, and I asked if it would be possible for a photo, to which he said "yes." That photo shows me grinning like a fool, but what I didn't realize at the time was that Dougherty was doing something to make the photo that much more memorable. Instead of a normal picture of Michael smiling, he twisted his face up in the most bizarre way which still has me laughing to this day. I have since met Dougherty two other times and both have left me with a feeling of happiness that is indescribable, as well as amazing photos where he makes the oddest, most hilarious expressions. They say you should never meet your heroes, but I'm thrilled to say that Mike is one of the good guys.

This past Halloween, I took the night off from work to watch the Collector's Edition of *Trick 'R Treat* and found that I had that goofy smile plastered on my face once again. Revisiting this movie with the knowledge that I would be writing about it for the first time left me feeling a tad overwhelmed as I didn't want to disappoint fans. Though I'm not known for being the most academic when it comes to my writing, I am known for writing from my heart with my emotions on full display. This movie means the world to me. These characters—no matter how nefarious or broken—mean so much to me. No one is the "hero." Instead each character shows their unsavory side, whether that be something as small as smashing pumpkins just to be an asshole or something as massive as a school-bus massacre. I bring this up not to draw attention to this side of humanity, but to remind people that we are all flawed individuals capable of making horrific choices, and as each of these characters learn, their choices come with disastrous consequences.

In 2018, this cult classic saw a resurgence in popularity when Halloween Horror Nights Orlando and Hollywood announced that they would both be designing mazes dedicated to the film. I, of course, traveled to both coasts so as to fully immerse myself in this world that Michael Dougherty created. To say it was a dream come true would be an understatement. I will admit that there were moments that almost made me shed a tear as I found myself in awe walking through the Rock Quarry, exploring Mr. Kreeg's house and discovering Sam on the ceiling, and even peeking in on Principal Wilkins feeding poisoned candy to a student.

Regardless of all the items I have collected over the years or the experiences that I have had, nothing will ever be as important as the first time I watched this film and the excitement over finally finding my "horror icon." Sure, my icon is in the form of a child-like pumpkin demon, but who's to judge? My love and appreciation for this film, for what Michael Dougherty created, and the central character that encompasses a large part of my life, will be something that follows me throughout the rest of my time on this planet. *Trick 'R Treat* is a reminder that there's nothing wrong with being the weird kid, celebrating All Hallow's Eve, and sticking to the traditions that make Halloween so important. I can only hope that I will be able to pass on my love for Halloween, Sam, and *Trick R' Treat* to others so they can see why this film has become an essential part of who I am.

Facing Your Fears

Learning To Love Home Invasion Horror Again After a Home Invasion

by Meredith Borders

IN FEBRUARY 2018, my husband and I woke in the middle of the night to find a man in our bedroom. Matt saw him first, this shape in the doorway, and he reached over to feel my side of the bed, hoping it would be empty, that the shape was just me. I woke up to my husband's hand on my arm, and somehow I knew, in those first few seconds, before I saw or heard anything, that someone who shouldn't be was in our room, our safest and most intimate space. The air felt wrong; the way my husband's hand was clutched around my forearm felt wrong. I looked over to the threshold of our room as slowly as I could, forcing my unwilling head to turn, and then I saw him, too.

It was several minutes before I could convince myself I was awake, that this wasn't a cold and precise dream that would stay with me for weeks. Even when I was on the phone with 911, I felt sure I was dreaming. Later, with a clearer head, I put together everything that had happened, and I realized that all of it took just forty minutes—forty minutes from waking to watching the police drive away with our invader in the back of their patrol car. It felt—it still feels—so much longer than that, this enormous thing that has irrevocably changed who I am, this powerful form that stands tall in the shadows of my mind, looking exactly like the shape of a skinny, silent man in the doorway of my bedroom. He wasn't armed. He was frightened, intoxicated, confused, and he didn't seem to be there to hurt us. My husband was with me and in control, cornering the man until the police arrived. Minutes later, they did. They arrested him—guns out, screaming at him to get down, and I remember crying over and over, "Don't shoot him, don't shoot him," so afraid they would kill this scared, scrawny interloper right in front of me. They left with him in handcuffs. We replaced the broken window he entered through and started locking our bedroom door, and we have never once forgotten to set our alarm since, the way we did that night in February.

I know how lucky I am. I wasn't alone that night. This man had no weapon. The police came quickly when we called. He never touched me. I am okay, and my husband is okay. But something inside me changed in those moments when I was finally able to convince myself that I wasn't dreaming, that there was a stranger in our bedroom, that I needed to be alert and aware and confront the situation in front of me. In those moments, though I didn't know it until later, I started to lose my love of being alone, and my love of being scared.

These have always been two of the most fundamental pieces of my character. One of my earliest memories is lying in my bed as a toddler, convincing myself that a shadow in the corner was a witch—not because I was scared, but because I *wasn't*, and I *wanted to be*. I have a bunch of siblings, and I spent most of my childhood trying to find a quiet nook to read in, an opportunity to be by myself with only my thoughts and someone else's words as company. Reading or watching horror by myself has been one of the chief joys of my life. "Yes, it's scary," I'd answer when people would ask me, "Isn't it scary to watch a horror movie by yourself?" Yes. It's scary. That's the point.

Twice in the month after the break-in, I became overcome with fear when left alone at night: in a hotel room during a work trip and dog-sitting at a friend's house while she was out of town. Both times I felt my heart start to clench as the sky grew darker. I began to feel a cold, weightless sensation in my hands and feet, a unique feeling I've always associated with anxiety and occasionally outright panic. I turned on all the lights, set absurd booby traps at bedroom doors, texted friends until all hours of the night, anything to keep myself from feeling alone, the very feeling I sought for so long. It seemed like such a loss, this newfound nervousness. I grieved my naivety of only four weeks before, when I was just one month younger, and had dealt with immense stress and anxiety and depression and personal disaster but never once felt unsafe the way I felt at that moment, sitting in a comfy guest room in a pretty townhouse in a well-lit neighborhood at barely 11 p.m. The idea of watching a horror film in those circumstances was suddenly unthinkable, and that felt like the greatest loss of all. It was a loss I could not abide.

So I set out to learn to love those two fundamental pieces of myself again. Forever a Type-A doer, I planned a regimen of fear for when I was alone. I started with books, because I've always been less viscerally affected by reading something scary rather than watching it. You're in control when you can simply close a book and set it aside, I reasoned, and of course that's also true of pausing a film, but it doesn't feel as safe and final to hit pause on a remote. Closing a book gives you that soft, satisfying clap that says, "That scary thing is gone now. It will be here when you're ready for it, but not until then."

I started with Michelle McNamara's stunning *I'll Be Gone in the Dark: One Woman's Obsessive Search for the Golden State Killer*. I chose to read the true and horrific stories of a man—alleged after publication to be former police officer Joseph James DeAngelo—breaking into the homes of women and couples, tying up the inhabitants, raping the women, his dozens of brutal crimes eventually escalating to serial murder. I read it when I was house-sitting alone. I listened to the audiobook while walking by myself at dusk. I read and listened in brief, adrenaline-charging bursts, taking breaks when I felt my heart racing and my breath growing short. I cried through a lot of *I'll Be Gone in the Dark*, for the women who died at the Golden State Killer's hands, for Michelle McNamara who put everything she had into writing this book and didn't live to see it published, for that woman I was a few weeks earlier, who never thought she'd wake to find a strange man in her bedroom, for the woman I am now who wakes several times every night expecting just that. And when I closed that book for the last time, after reading McNamara's beautiful and furious "Letter to an Old Man," I felt a little less afraid.

It's paradoxical, maybe, that reading about such real, actual horror, stories a hundred thousand times worse than my own, would make me feel stronger, but it did. I survived what happened to me, and I survived reading this book so soon after. Dozens of women survived the attacks of the Golden State Killer. Women survive. It's what we do. It's a thought I clung to, though embarrassed to be equating my own, small story to those so much more devastating and consequential, and in truth I'm embarrassed still. But that equation, unjust as it may be, helped me.

So I moved on to a novel, Lauren Beukes' *The Shining Girls*, about a time-traveling serial killer who stalks and kills extraordinary women in their own once-safe spaces. Beukes breaks from murder fiction form by focusing on the women this killer targets, treating them not as bloody fodder but as singular, complicated, shining examples of humanity. I read it on my porch at night by myself, trying to ignore the panic in my chest as a neighbor walked by my yard and glanced in at me. I cried, again, for the shining girls, and I had nightmares and anxiety attacks and closed the book many, many times. And when I finished reading it, I felt a little less afraid.

I was ready for movies. I rewatched *The Strangers* (2008) first. My heart broke for James and Kristen, who never got to find closure from their breakup, because Kristen's rejection of James' proposal was so soon followed by that knock on the door. I was most moved by Kristen's obstinate disbelief as masked invaders take over the house, the way she kept saying "no," rejecting the reality of what's happening to her. I understood that soul-deep rejection of a situation that must instead be confronted. I've felt it myself.

Next I watched *Funny Games* (2007), struggling with Ann and George as they try desperately to deny the sadistic games their captors are forcing on them. I watched *Wait Until Dark* (1967) for the first time since high school, marveling at Susy's immeasurable strength and cleverness. I rewatched *You're Next* (2011) and found that movie less funny and more terrifying than I've ever found it before. I cracked open my old *Inside* (2007) DVD, and wondered if this would be the last time I'd be able to bring myself to watch that once-favorite film.

Every time a shape emerged from the shadows, like *Inside*'s La Femme taking gradual form in the dark behind an unwitting Sarah, I'd forget to breathe. Shapes in doorways used to feel like cheap jump scares; now they resonate down to my guts, an instant, icy shorthand back to that night. But I'm nearly as affected by reflections in mirrors, killers around corners, silhouettes moving quickly in the background. These narrative tricks used to do nothing to me, or at best they'd elicit a startled chuckle, and now each one frightens me to my core. And maybe that's okay, I started to realize. After all, being scared during scary movies is why we're all here, right? I'm a cheaper date now, so to speak, when it comes to horror movies. I get more bang for my buck. I'm no longer academically appreciating these films from a safe distance. I'm feeling what I'm supposed to feel when I watch them. And I guess that's not such a bad thing.

I cried at least once during every one of these movies. They gave me nightmares and insomnia, heightened anxiety, even paranoia at times. Sometimes I didn't know why I was making myself watch and read these things. It felt like a dare to myself, a cruel punishment for someone else's crime. But I knew that I had to push through the worst of this exercise and stumble onto the other side as *myself*, and *myself* is someone who loves to be afraid, who cherishes being alone. Maybe it was a dare, but not one born out of punishment. I was daring myself out of pride, pride for who I once was and was determined to be again.

And when each movie was over, I felt a little less afraid.

I'm still not sure why it works, why scaring myself is turning me into less of a scaredy-cat. I guess it's because every time I watch a horror film or read a scary book by myself, I'm proving that I can do it, even if I don't quite yet *want* to do it. I might still be checking every closet and corner twice before going to bed at night, but I'm also being active, making a deliberate decision to scare myself instead of passively allowing the fear to sneak up on me when I'm not ready for it, like when our air conditioner clicks on or the dog steps on a creaky floorboard. This fear is my choice, and making that choice feels a little bit like strength.

I wish I had a tidy resolution for this journey. I wish I could tell you, "I love horror again, and I love being alone." I'm not there yet. As I'm writing this, I am alone. The sun is setting soon, and my heart rate is already a little faster. My hands are starting to feel a bit cold and floaty. I'm scared, still, but pushing through it. I know my bedroom will never feel safe again. My home will never again be my haven. At times I hate the sight of it. I want to make this house collapse in on itself like Carrie's after the prom. My sleep will never be as peaceful as it once was. But I won't let that night take from me what I love best in this world. It changed me, but I can change myself, too.

Cheap Scares: The Startle Effect and Community

by Sonia Lupher

> *"Psycho is a film made with quite a sense of amusement on my part. To me it's a fun picture. The processes through which we take the audience, you see, it's rather like taking them through the haunted house at the fairground."*
>
> –Alfred Hitchcock

LIKE MANY HORROR FANS, I have a conflicted relationship with the "jump scare" or startle effect. On one hand, it is tempting to call them "cheap" scares because they are often dismissed as uninspired, derivative, and a last resort to render a film scary when nothing else works—premise, suspense, or atmosphere. When I see a new horror movie with friends, inevitably one expresses the hope that it will not be "just a bunch of jump scares"—that the films will provide substance, rather than fleeting frights.

This dismissal of the startle effect recalls a primary argument against the horror film's cultural value: that it exploits bodily reactions, rather than inciting intellectual engagement. As John Kenneth Muir has written, the jump scare is often disparaged because it targets an "involuntary human response."[1] Robert Baird similarly suggests that the technique is under-appreciated because it "represents the most extreme form of sensationalism, a stark contract with the ideals of *art* and *thought*."[2]

---

1. Muir, John Kenneth. *Horror Films FAQ: All That's Left to Know About Slashers, Vampires, Zombies, Aliens, and More.* Milwaukee, WI: Applause Cinema and Theatre Books, 2013.

2. Baird, Robert. "The Startle Effect: Implications for Spectator Cognition and Media Theory." *Film Quarterly*, vol. 53, no. 3, Spring 2000, pp. 12-24.

Because it is fleeting and so centralized on the body, the jump scare is easily dismissed as anti-intellectual, cheap, and distasteful—a "trick" on the audience.

When I watched horror films alone as a teen, I would often fast-forward when I suspected that a jump scare was about to happen, then rewind and watch the scene with my ears covered. This impulse has never entirely left me. Although I do consider myself a horror fan, and I seek out films that will shock and frighten me, I still cover my ears when I anticipate a jump scare (especially in a theater). I do not enjoy being startled. On the other hand, experiencing a jump scare in a crowded theatre mirrors the thrill of a rollercoaster ride; it is, simply put, fun to be frightened with an audience.

The jump scare is interesting for several different reasons. It is distinctive in its varying degrees of effectiveness—for instance, and with few exceptions, the sound and image must be carefully choreographed in order to inspire the intended response. While not all audiences may experience suspense or atmosphere in the same way, the horror genre is unique in exploiting the universal impulse to be startled. In this essay, I will consider selected jump scares from two different films, Takashi Shimizu's *The Grudge* (2004) and Scott Derrickson's *Sinister* (2012), to make a case for the jump scare's unique function of enabling a communal fright, particularly (but not necessarily) in a movie theater setting.

Many who write on the jump scare tend to focus on its cognitive or physical process; Robert Fuoco is among the few who approach the subject in terms of aesthetics. Baird, for instance, refers to psychological studies that document how people react to being startled. Many of these studies also associate a person's likelihood to be startled with their concurrent emotional states: "large startle responses are potentiated by aversive emotion—notably the fear state."[3] Ronald R. Simons, who wrote among the only book-length studies of the startle effect (though without an emphasis on film) confirms that it is an evolutionary response, universal to all animals and species, and serves a primal "first respond, then assess"[4] purpose. He points out that while reactions to the startle effect vary culturally, its utilitarian purpose renders it "a relatively apolitical subject." Muir and Noël Carroll separately agree. Carroll writes

---

3. Vrana, Scott R. & Peter J. Lang. "Fear Imagery and the Startle-Probe Reflex." *Journal of Abnormal Psychology*, vol. 99, no. 2, 1990, pp. 187-197.

4. Simons, Ronald C. *Boo! Culture, Experience, and the Startle Reflex*. Oxford: Oxford University Press, 1996.

that the startle effect in film is, "in certain respects, beyond politics and ideology,"[5] while Muir identifies it as one element among three that illustrate how horror films scare audiences. The other two elements he names are film grammar—how the film is shot—and the subject matter, "where history, politics, and economics come into the picture" to make a socially relevant statement that audiences, presumably, can identify with.

Writing from a philosophical standpoint, Alexandre Declos discusses the relationship between surprise and artistic innovation. Surprise, he argues, always "[correlates] with a judgment of value."[6] Artists who surprise their audience are often seen as breaking new ground by "making us think and feel in a new way." The apparent paradox here is that filmmakers who rely on the startle effect are often seen as derivative and formulaic, even as the startle effect never fails to have its desired effect (even on repeated viewings). As Philip Brophy writes, "the cheapest trick in the book will still tense your muscles, quicken your heart and jangle your nerves."[7] In film, the startle effect might better align with Declos' definition of "the unexpected," which he distinguishes from surprise. While the latter relies on an individual having their expectations thwarted, something unexpected is "a purely emotional and reflex reaction... when we were not expecting *anything* at all." The cinematic jump scare, however, seem to contradict both Declos' definition of surprise and the unexpected. While seasoned viewers *do* expect jump scares and often identify the aesthetic patterns that precede them (a drop in volume on the soundtrack, for instance), they still react to the scare in the intended way.

Like Muir, many critics argue that jump scares alone do not guarantee an effective horror film (though "effective" is a difficult evaluative statement to make). Mike Jones, for instance, claims that for a horror film to fulfill its "contractual obligations" of scaring the audience, it must employ "shock, dread, anxiety, and terror;" in discussing the first in detail, he argues that shock "represents the most blunt, albeit effective, of

---

5. Carroll, Noël. "Prospects for Film Theory: A Personal Assessment." In *Post-Theory: Reconstructing Film Studies*. Eds. David Bordwell & Noël Carroll. Madison: University of Wisconsin Press, 2012.

6. Declos, Alexandre. "The Aesthetic and Cognitive Value of Surprise." *Proceedings of the European Society for Aesthetics*, vol. 6, 2014, pp. 1-18.

7. Brophy, Philip. "Horrality: The Textuality of Contemporary Horror Films." In *The Horror Reader*. Ed. Ken Gelder. New York: Routledge, 2000.

cinematic scare devices" because it never fails to exploit our evolutionary reflexes.[8] Pedro Asdrubal Diaz contends that a well-executed plot should be enough to elicit scares from its audience. Equating jump scares with a lack of creativity, he asks, "sure, you jump and scream during the movie, but does it stick with you?" Diaz is making two problematic assumptions here. First, that there are two qualitative poles—the bad one (jumping and screaming) and the good one (lasting fright). Second, he implies that jump scares do not stick with a viewer. His question reminds me of seeing *Sinister 2* (2015) in the movie theater with two friends who had loved the original. One friend remembered just one jump scare in *Sinister*. In his mind, therefore, the film had seemed to rely on other, less momentary scare tactics that had stayed with him longer. The other friend, his fiancée, agreed and compared her experience of seeing *Sinister* and *The Conjuring* (2013). Even though she had reacted more physically to *The Conjuring*, she claimed that *Sinister* had "stayed" with her the longest, "unsettled" her for several days following, and that, for that reason, it was "more of a horror film."

Their mutual appreciation for *Sinister*'s lack of reliance on jump scares alluded to a binary between the superficial, "cheap" scare and the genuine, bone-chilling, never-sleep-again horror. This also pits the immediate experience of seeing the film against that of remembering the film later. Inside and outside the viewing experience, the film becomes a different product altogether, either one that was "not actually scary" in retrospect or one that "sticks."

In actuality, *Sinister* employs numerous jump scares, at least three frequently cited ones and several more minor ones. But my friends' experience suggests that the memory of being startled during a horror film is often skewed in retrospect and that, in turn, startling moments in horror films are just that—moments—and until they are analyzed, they are likely to be misremembered. The two scenes I will discuss were ones I remembered as being completely silent, and upon revisiting them I was surprised to find that both are accompanied by loud, startling *bangs* on the soundtrack that mirror how I had remembered the shock of unexpectedly seeing a ghostly face in each film. Furthermore, both of the jump scares I will discuss *did* "stick" with me; I remembered them chillingly long afterward. Even so, because they rely on the experience of disorientation (our body reacts; our mind assesses), the likelihood

---

8. Jones, Mike. "Shock Horror: Genre, Audience and the anatomy of Fear." *Screen Education*, issue 65, 2011, pp. 96-106.

that jump scares will be misremembered increases and the fact of their momentary effectiveness is reinforced.

The Grudge is a remake of Shimizu's 2002 Japanese-language film of the same name (*Ju-On: The Grudge*). The 2004 remake is also set in Tokyo, and it features the same two actors who play the vengeful ghosts, Kayako (Takako Fuji) and Toshio (Yuya Ozeki) of the original, a mother and son who were murdered by Kayako's jealous husband. The titular grudge refers to a curse that manifests itself when someone is violently murdered, and in both films the grudge haunts a house where Emma (Grace Zabriskie in the remake), a woman with dementia, lives alone.

Among the 2004 film's protagonists is Karen Davis (Sarah Michelle Gellar), a caregiver who replaces the nurse who mysteriously disappears after being assigned to Emma's care. During her first visit with Emma, Karen encounters Toshio, his cat (also a ghost), and Kayako, the latter of whom emits only prolonged guttural croaking, a "death rattle" (it is later revealed that her neck was broken when she was murdered). Suffering from shock, Karen is admitted to a hospital. When she is released, her boyfriend Doug (Jason Behr) takes her home on the bus. Karen sits by the window, looking troubled, and Doug asks what's bothering her. Karen responds that she is plagued with thoughts of her visit with Emma (who died when Kayako appeared) and the "thing" she saw. "I think I saw something in that house," she says. The creaking bus and the whizzing of passing bicycles can also be heard on the soundtrack. Karen continues, "Emma and I were alone in that room, but I think there was something else there with us." As soon as she finishes the line, the ambient croaks and revving of passing cycles turns into the guttural growl of Kayako's punctured vocal chords as she appears in the reflection of the bus window. The ghostly apparition and accompanying sound anticipates the swell of the soundtrack to a high-pitched bang meant to emulate Karen's shock.

The shock reverberates into a rhythmic pulsing on the soundtrack, along with a long, shrill note on violins, which are finally joined by the notes of a calmer, but still high-pitched, piano theme as Karen calms down. A reverse shot shows Karen reflected vividly in the bus window, suggesting that she may have mistaken her reflection for that of the ghost. This jump scare is designed to match Karen's startled reaction to what she sees (or thinks she sees) in the reflection of the bus window. The creaking sounds of the bus and passing vehicles transform quickly, and purposefully, to recall the ghost's croak as her face appears, while the *bang* on the soundtrack ensures that the audience will react in a way that mirrors Karen's fright.

Like *The Grudge,* the threat in *Sinister* is supernatural: not a ghost, but the fictional Babylonian demon Bughuul, "devourer of children," who has found the 8mm camera a useful contemporary medium for facilitating his nefarious activities. The film follows true crime writer Ellison Oswalt (Ethan Hawke), as he researches a case about a murdered family and their missing child. In order to work more closely with the crime scene, Ellison moves his wife and two children into the very house where the killings occurred; his wife, Tracy (Juliet Rylance) is ignorant to this grisly fact.

Through 8mm footage he finds in the attic, Ellison connects the case to other similar ones across the country—all of them involving a murdered family and a missing child. As he pieces together the crimes and begins to learn about Bughuul, Ellison experiences several unnerving occurrences at nighttime, while he works and his family sleeps. When he hears a mysterious sound one night, Ellison takes a baseball bat and creeps through his house, checking rooms and hallways for the source. The scene is mostly silent, apart from the creaking of Ellison's footsteps and a vague, low note on the soundtrack. The film cuts from a medium-long shot on Ellison's back as he looks into the kitchen to a close-up of his face as he turns his head from the left of the screen. The entire right half of the screen is dark, but as soon as Ellison peers in that direction, a young, blonde girl's decomposing face plunges abruptly into the right side of the frame, along with a loud bang on the soundtrack (percussion and strings). Ellison's expression remains unchanged; clearly, he does not see her, and the soundtrack begins to wane as the camera cuts back to a medium-long shot that shows Ellison turning away from the young girl, who is standing on the dining room table and leaning forward to look intently after him. In slow motion, she runs and leaps off the table as Ellison begins to leave the room. He reacts to the creak of her landing, but still fails to see her.

As Ellison continues to check the rest of the house, other ghostly children appear in turn and move around Ellison, alternately running toward him and away from him. Like the first girl, they move in slow motion that suggests they inhabit a different (ghostly) spatial and temporal existence that can touch the boundary of Ellison's world but cannot cross it. The sudden appearance of a girl in a yellow raincoat is also accompanied by a bang on the soundtrack as the camera cuts to a closer shot on her, but the first girl delivers the largest shock. Because Ellison never sees the figures, this scene is notable for its intention to frighten the audience alone.

Baird and others discuss the jump scare in terms of its mirroring function—it allows the audience to experience what a character feels when startled. Jones argues that a jump scare "directly relies upon the viewer knowing only what the character being scared knows." While this is often the case, the afore-described scene from *Sinister* is an example of a jump scare designed entirely to frighten the audience, independent of what the character sees. And as many critics note, the jump scare remains overwhelmingly popular among horror fans. Bryan Bishop writes, "it's clear audiences appreciate a well-tuned jump"[9] while Baird suggests that "the only groups not afraid of startle appear to be film viewers and makers, whose appreciation of the effect remains strong."

Val Lewton, the horror film producer often credited as among the first to regularly employ jump scares in his films (most famously the bus scene in *Cat People* [1942]), was known for attending sneak previews of his films, where "he sat in the back and witnessed an entire audience jumping in unison at the appropriate time."[10] Perhaps Lewton's pleasure at watching an audience react to his carefully plotted jump scares was sadistic, but it also reinforces the temporal limits of the jump scare technique. In an article about Hitchcock's *Psycho* (1960) and its initial audiences, Linda Williams credits the film with launching the spectator's desire to be "thrilled and moved in quite visceral ways"[11] that remains a primary concern of contemporary horror filmmaking and viewing. Williams describes *Psycho*'s first audiences as experiencing, through the shock and rollercoaster-like ride that changed so much about film spectatorship (not least the "discipline" of being required to show up at the theater on time), a "camaraderie, a pleasure of the group" that has since then become a staple of the horror film viewing experience.

Whether horror films are viewed in the theater or at home, the jump scare is unique in its ability to elicit a reaction from anybody. With its clear lead-up and anticipation, it requires horror film audiences to be

---

9. https://www.theverge.com/2012/10/31/3574592/art-of-the-jump-scare-horror-movies

10. Bansak, Edmund G. *Fearing the Dark: The Val Lewton Career*. North Carolina: McFarland & Company, Inc., 1995.

11. Williams, Linda. "Discipline and Fun: *Psycho* and Postmodern Cinema." In *Reinventing Film Studies*. Eds. Christine Gledhill & Linda Williams. London: Arnold, 2000.

disciplined (viewing the screen, engaging at least minimally in the story) in order to reap the benefits (or heart attack) of the resulting fright-turned-relief.

The Therapeutic Benefits of Horror for Those Suffering with Illness

by BJ Colangelo

NEARLY FIVE YEARS AGO, I walked into a Cleveland emergency room with symptoms of acid-reflux disease and was quickly moved from room to room, doctor to doctor, and test to test. Acid-reflux I did not have, but pancreatic cancer, I did. The reality is this: I am living with a disease that has a four percent survival rate. Statistically speaking, ninety-six percent of the other people that battle pancreatic cancer pass away after five years. The fact I am still alive is nothing short of a miracle.

Following my initial diagnosis, a team of doctors removed a tennis ball-sized pancreatic tumor, forty percent of my pancreas, my entire spleen, and lymph nodes. Upon further examination, cancer was present in the lymph nodes located closest to the site of my tumor. My doctors legitimately caught the cancer as it was starting to spread throughout my body.

As could be expected, I spent a long time in the hospital, and I've spent the last five years enduring radiation and recovery. When I was diagnosed at twenty-three years old, there was a forty percent chance of the cancer returning, but my doctors even admitted that it was an arbitrary guess as the statistics on pancreatic cancer are based on previous cases. As pancreatic cancer is a somewhat symptomless disease, people traditionally aren't diagnosed until much later in life. During my hospital stay, I was the youngest patient on my floor by at least twenty years. Only two years after I was legally able to drink a glass of wine at dinner, I was forced to accept the very real and distinct possibility that I'll show up to a doctor's appointment only to be told that I'm going to die.

Dr. Phillip K. Decker in *Nightbreed* (1990) encompasses exactly how it feels to be fighting a severe illness: "Quite a dance, huh? Death everywhere, and you and me in the middle." When you're fighting a severe illness, every single aspect of your life is dictated by said illness. Can you go to the store and have the mental capacity to endure stares from other patrons? Should you wash your hair today, or is it just going to make more of it fall out? Are the spices you add to your food in order to actually taste *something* going to be worth the awful stomach pains you'll have later? When you're sick, you lose all sense of autonomy. I've always prided myself on being a strong person, but nothing makes you feel more vulnerable than something like cancer.

Horror movies have always had a place in my life as a sense of comfort, but that cathartic release was only heightened after diagnosis. From my initial emergency room visit to the entire hospital stay and now in recovery, my media consumption has been dominated by horror movies.

Watching horror elicits uncontrolled responses both mentally and physically. Your heart rate quickens, a sense of fight or flight is immediately triggered, anxiety heightens, and your body releases a rush of adrenaline throughout your veins. All of these sensations are also present when dealing with an illness, but the difference is that a horror film allows you to process these emotions and feelings from a safe and fictional distance. What horror offers that illness does not, however, is the release of dopamine. During the adrenaline rush and fight-or-flight impulse, your body also releases dopamine, which is a hormone that triggers the reward centers of the brain giving you a positive feeling.

This observation from my own personal experience isn't biased; it's actually backed by science and psychology. In an interview with *Vice*,[1] Dr. Mathias Clasen from Aarhus University in Denmark spoke to Abby Moss stating, "Exposure to horror films can be gratifying when the negative emotions caused by the film are manageable." Dr. Clasen is considered one of the most brilliant minds in this field and has been studying the psychological effects of horror movies for over fifteen years. He continued to explain, saying, "Moreover, there's psychological distance when we watch a horror film. We know it's not real—or at least, some parts of our

---

1. https://broadly.vice.com/en_us/article/a3wdzk/why-some-anxious-people-find-comfort-in-horror-movies

brain know it isn't real. Other parts—ancient structures located in the limbic system—respond as though it were real."

The benefits of watching horror films aren't just psychological, they're physically beneficial as well. Back in 2003, the journal *Stress* published a study from Coventry University in the United Kingdom, which noted that watching a horror film significantly increased people's levels of disease- and infection-fighting white blood cells. Meaning, watching a horror film offers a temporary jolt to the immune system, something that ill people desperately need.

It's important to note that this sort of cathartic release is not for everyone. There are plenty that find exposure to horror actually heightens their fears or their anxieties, but for many of us, this seemingly unconventional method of therapy can have tremendous benefits. This phenomenon I'm discussing is not one that's meant to be viewed as a professional medical treatment, but rather an analysis of something that has worked for myself and others in my position. As always, if you think you are currently suffering from any type of illness, please seek professional help from a licensed doctor, therapist, or psychiatrist.

Margee Kerr, a sociologist and fear researcher and author of *Scream: Chilling Adventures In the Science of Fear* noted that these benefits only exist for willing participants for fear. If you're consciously choosing to participate in being scared, the benefits await. If you're forcing someone into being afraid, the results are actually completely in the contrary.

Unlike being diagnosed with an illness, watching a horror film offers us a controlled environment to voluntarily process these negative feelings. There's an immense sense of helplessness when you're sick because the outcome is completely out of your control. Sure, there's the mindset that having a positive attitude helps with healing, but unless you're a doctor actually performing a surgery or coming up with the chemical concoction to kill the dastardly cells, there's not really much you can do to expedite the healing or recovery process. You're forced to deal with this negative circumstance whether you want to or not. Watching a horror film establishes that lost sense of control.

Despite its century-long popularity in Western civilization, openly admitting to enjoying horror films is frequently viewed as "lesser-than" by the general public. However, when you're living in a hospital, it becomes an identifiable personality trait. My nursing staff was already relieved to have a patient under the age of thirty, which meant I could crack jokes with them at all hours of the day, but the fact I loved horror movies was something very unique to me. Playing a new horror film in my room every time my nurses arrived during their rounds gave them a reason to talk to me about things other than my illness. Quoting alongside Quint meant my nurses could talk to me about sharks and their own personal experiences with seeing the *Jaws* (1975) for the first time, and for just a moment, we talked about being afraid of something that wasn't the cancer raging through my body.

While all films offer audiences the ability to transport themselves into a world that isn't their own, horror has always offered the ultimate in escapism. When you're suffering from a severe illness, that escapism isn't just desirable, it's mandatory. For sick people, everyone around you is either crying or filled with a forced positive attitude. Doctors and nurses are constantly telling you what to do to survive, or commenting on anything remotely positive, no matter how menial, in an attempt to offer a positive attitude. For me, personally, my parents were painfully retelling the updates on my condition over and over and over to anyone that called, and I had more social media notifications than on my birthday. Being the center of attention like that is exhausting. If I had to hear "how are you feeling?" one more time, I was going to rip out my IV and stab someone with it.

All I wanted to do was scream or blow everyone's heads off and since I couldn't do that, I watched it on screen. There was something incredibly therapeutic about watching other people literally tear off their skin when all you wanted to do was live inside someone else's. It's a hell of a lot easier to forget you're dying when you're watching other people do it in front of your eyes. Watching someone other than you suffer in a movie allows you to accept the realities of your own situation.

Historically speaking, in practices like exposure therapy for phobias, individuals are frequently exposed to their fear to slowly become desensitized and no longer associate negative outcomes with that fear. When you're at risk of dying, seeing death over and over again helps make that fear of death manageable. For me, it helped to see the pain and terror I was feeling personified on film. It permitted my anxiety to come out, be acknowledged, and socially comforted.

Writer Patricia Grisafi wrote in an essay for *LunaLuna Magazine*, "Coping with real world situations is sometimes intolerable for people with sensitive nervous systems." She continued saying, "Dulling our senses with inexplicable horror and violence just might help a disordered nervous system become more amenable to the everyday crises of life."

Every single person alive is afraid of something, and for a majority of us, reckoning with our own mortality is a huge part of it. When you're suffering from an illness, facing mortality isn't a fear, it's just another thing on the list of things to do every day. One of the ultimate and universal appeals of horror films is the desire to see someone survive despite tremendous odds and uncertainty. We identify with the Final Girl in a slasher film because we too believe we could endure and overcome the same circumstances.

The more popular horror films—slasher films in particular—serve as morality stories with poetic justice. Horror frequently rewards all of the virtues of living a healthy lifestyle, something that can be extremely cathartic for someone with a severe illness. We're constantly dealing with the fact that our situation is anything but fair.

I spent the first two weeks screaming "why me?" and feeling sorry for myself, and I wasn't wrong in feeling that this wasn't fair. Life isn't fair, but horror movies usually are. People like me survive, and when you're actually dying, that sort of ideal shown in the media makes a world of difference. We shouldn't need a masked slasher to improve the state of America's healthcare system, but one certainly would help.

Sometimes things happen in life that are uglier and more horrific than anything we can imagine, and while some people may crave hope and Nicholas Sparks movies, there are many of us who want something to scare us that isn't coming out of a biopsy. For me, I want something to take me out of the terror that is very, very real and allow me to feel sad, scared, and angry at something other than myself. I don't want to watch my mom cry in my hospital room because she can't save her child; I want to watch Katherine Thorn struggle with raising the anti-Christ in *The Omen* (1976). I don't want to look at the hideous surgery scar on my stomach; I want to watch James Woods pull a gun out of his guts in *Videodrome* (1983).

Ultimately, the greatest benefit for people suffering from illnesses watching horror is the sense of schadenfreude. In our daily lives, we are the people that all of our friends look to as being in the worst possible situation. If our loved ones are having a bad day at their jobs or in their personal lives, they look to our situations as the staple of "well, it could always be worse." When you're dying, where are we supposed to look for any sign that we're not in the trenches with no possibility of recovering?

Horror movies.

We'll always have horror movies.

Monsters: Horror's Most Human Creatures

by Jennica Lynn

It was a blazing hot summer day in Northern Californian suburbia, and I hadn't yet adjusted to the dryness or the dehydration or the exhaustion induced by hours of outdoor activities with the neighbor children. I had just moved to the upper half of the state with my family two years prior and despite relocating to a town only a few hundred miles from what I had formerly called home, my adaptation began as an environmental shock. Not an ounce of moisture in the air, not a beach in sight, and no dark corner was left uninhabited by arachnids with varying degrees of lethality.

After much perspiring under the brutal sun, I had reached a level of physical fatigue that I had never before known as an eight year old girl. I shuffled into my new childhood home dragging one foot in front of the other. I dropped to the floor, curled into a fetal position, and quickly drifted into a deep mid-day slumber. Upon gradual return to consciousness, I felt a subtle tingling sensation across my cheek as if a hair—or several hairs—had brushed against my skin. As I came to a stronger awareness of my surroundings, the tingling better resembled light, but insistent tapping.

When I opened my eyes, there were no hairs, and I had forgotten the tickling, tingling feeling as I was shaken by the sight of eight thin black legs dancing down my face and onto the floor. I laid there ever so still as I watched the beady-eyed invader make its escape to the other side of the room. I couldn't move; I couldn't even scream. That day, I experienced genuine fear as I saw my first real-life monster.

WHAT IS A MONSTER?

Often when we think about monsters, we envision legendary creatures such as the sphinx, the centaur, or the literary-based Cthulhu. We also habitually look to the silver screen for vampires, werewolves, and mummies. Of course, these are all standard examples of monsters. But how can we define the word "monster?"

According to Lisa Wenger Bro and Crystal O'Leary-Davison et al., authors of *Monsters of Film, Fiction, and Fable,* monsters contain the following five traits that set them apart from humans:

- Inspiring fear/horror
- Unnatural/abnormal
- Evil/immoral
- Uncivilized/savage
- Chaotic

The problem with this definition of monsters is that it is too limiting in its assumption that only fantastical beings can have these traits. Horror films have frequently implied that humans may be the greatest monsters of all. Many of these films have reflected actual political conflicts and flaws in our social system throughout history. We are all capable of displaying each one of the above traits, but our history and experiences as rational beings are evidence that what we fear is likely determined by how we define the latter four traits. Thus, I propose that a monster should instead be defined as anything that we fear *because* we believe it to be unnatural/abnormal, evil/immoral, uncivilized/savage, and chaotic.

INNATE VERSUS LEARNED FEAR

This new definition of monster then leaves us with the question of how we decide what is unnatural/abnormal, evil/immoral, uncivilized/savage, and chaotic. How did we decide that a fictional character such as Frankenstein's monster, a man-made creature desiring the love of another, is evil? Returning to my creepy crawly trauma, how did I conclude spiders—living things that are a part of nature—are unnatural and a threat to my safety? Is fear and the belief that someone or something is inherently bad an innate trait or a learned behavior?

In a recent study by neurologist Stefanie Hoehl at the University of Vienna, it was discovered that infants as young as six months old responded in an alarmed manner to pictures of spiders and snakes compared to pictures of flowers and fish, suggesting that certain fears of living things that our ancestors believed to be monstrous beasts is hardwired for the sake of survival.[1] There are many snakes and spiders that are poisonous, which makes a natural fear and avoidance of them appear logical. The belief that it is better to make generalizations than to take a chance on the unknown seems to be a common thought process in the human brain. Categorization is the easiest way to make a fast decision. Flowers good. Spiders bad.

On the contrary, this theory of innate fear can be quickly refuted in another study, which explains that there is a reason that films such as *Big Ass Spider!* (2013) and *Snakes on a Plane* (2006) continue to achieve a cult following. This new study published in *Current Directions in Psychological Science* in 2011, a popular journal affiliated with the Association for Psychological Science, claims that infants can quickly learn to fear spiders and snakes depending on the way in which these so-called monsters are introduced.[2] For example, when infants were shown videos of spiders or snakes and heard the sound of a cheerful voice, they did not display signs of fear versus when viewing these videos with the sounds of a frightened voice. This suggests that social cues are a deciding factor in what we fear and what we categorize as monstrous or bad.

Monsters and Conformity

Learned fear is not exclusive to other species, but can be extended to our friends, family, and neighbors. We can be taught to fear our fellow man and woman with minimal cause as long as there is an authoritative majority with a shared opinion that pushes "groupthink," a psychology term defined by decisions made as a group in such a manner that discourage individuality and encourage anonymity. It was the angry villagers that truly made Frankenstein's monster into an abomination. We did not see anyone putting down their torch and pitchfork to raise

---

1. Pappas, S. *Live Science,* October 20, 2007. "Baby Arachnophobia: Tots' Fear of Spiders and Snakes May Be Innate."

2. LoBlue, V. *Current Directions in Psychological Science* January 24, 2011. "People Aren't Born Afraid of Spiders and Snakes: Fear Is Quickly Learned During Infancy."

concerns before marching through the town as they likely feared that they would be chastised along with the monster. The need for acceptance and belonging are universal.

Outside of the realm of fictional tales, students at Stanford University witnessed what was supposed to be a simulated situation involving groupthink in 1971 when Professor Phillip Zimbardo conducted an experiment in the Psychology Department basement to study prison behavior. In the beginning, nine students were "arrested," read their rights, searched, and led down a hallway to their designated "prison cells" while nine other students were assigned as prison guards. Each prisoner was given a uniform with an ID number and would only be addressed by their number, creating instant anonymity. The guards were given identical wardrobes with no instruction other than to demand order and respect.

As rebellion began to break out in the made-up prison after one day, the guards designated "good" cells and "bad" cells, creating a divide and distrust among the prisoners. When prisoner #819 continued to rebel, he was humiliated by the guards with the help of the "good" prisoners, continuously repeating "Prisoner #819 did a bad thing… prisoner #819 did a bad thing… prisoner #819 did a bad thing…" until both the guards, the "good" prisoners, and even prisoner #819 believed that he was "bad." This type of behavior can be found in horror films from *Frankenstein* (1931) to *The Thing* (1982) to *Starry Eyes* (2014). It is also in plain view within horrific moments in history such as the Nazis following Adolf Hitler's orders during the Holocaust and American conservatives siding with Donald Trump's demands to keep Mexican immigrants from entering the supposedly free world. Perhaps the conformists—the creators of monsters—are also monsters themselves, as they could just as easily be unnatural/abnormal, evil/immoral, uncivilized/savage, and chaotic through the eyes of the monsters that they have created.

Taking this idea of learned fear from conformity and groupthink a step further, there have been many real and fictional events that have pointed toward conformity as the very creator of monsters in film and society; it is the blueprint for what is considered to be natural/normal, good/moral, civilized, and orderly. Anything outside the social, political, and moral values of the majority is cast out as a threat, as misunderstood, as a monster… and the values of the majority are ever evolving.

Monsters Before Movies

Before the invention of moving pictures, monsters were rearing their ugly heads in religious texts, urban legends and folklore, and fictional novels, many of these stemming from Christianity and Freudian psychoanalysis. For centuries, conformity in many regions of the world could be defined as abiding by the biblical rules of morality, particularly the belief that only God can create man (and woman).

As early as 975 AD, the very first manuscript was developed for *Beowulf*, perhaps one of the oldest tales of a monster created by a conformist disguised as a hero. Taking place in Scandinavia, the hero of the story, Beowulf, assists King Hrothgar, whose feasting hall in his palace has been invaded nightly by a monster called Grendel, the son of Cain, Christianity's first murderer. After Beowulf kills him, Grendel's mother attacks the grounds and, like her son, is also destroyed. Triumphant and possibly narcissistic, Beowulf returns to his home and he is promoted to a king. Years later, Beowulf conquers a dragon but dies from a gruesome battle wound. His followers then burn his remains and construct a monument in his honor.

In his book *On Monsters: An Unnatural History of Our Worst Fears*, Stephen T. Asma explains that initially monsters such as Grendel are considered "outcasts *because* they are bad." The original textual telling of Beowulf and Grendel emphasizes that the alleged monster, Grendel, is guilty by association with his killer father who defied the Commandment "love thy neighbor." Grendel's destruction of King Hrothgar's palace only demonstrates a self-fulfilling prophecy, leading to Asma's later, more liberal, observation that perhaps monsters in reality and in fiction are "bad *because* they are outcasts."

Self-fulfilling prophecy, no matter how conformity is defined in each decade, has been a continued theme for us as social creatures. It is the power of self-fulfilling prophecy that sometimes reveals the heroes and creators of villains as monsters themselves.

For example, as previously discussed, Frankenstein's monster was not physically built to be a threat to society but was primed by Dr. Frankenstein to lack an understanding of what it is to be loved. With the villagers crying "monster" without a second thought, the poor green giant didn't have a cold chance in Hell at acceptance. Dr. Frankenstein calls his creation "wretched devil," "daemon," a "vile insect." The villagers only see the creature as an act of science against God, an abomination. Because

Frankenstein's monster was treated as a monster from the start, he only did what he believed a monster would do.

Such stories as *Beowulf* and Mary Shelley's *Frankenstein* were only the beginning of what University of Notre Dame, Australia's Senior Lecturer in Philosophy Laura D'Olimpio describes as "a time in which we see a fear of otherness manifest in discrimination, hatred, and exclusion."[3]

UNIVERSAL MONSTERS AND UNIVERSAL FEARS

Leaping from the pages of books to the silver screen, conformity expanded from mere biblical morality to patriotism and Americanization. Twelve years after World War I, three years after the notorious 1929 stock market crash, and at the peak of Central European fascism, Eastern European Communism and an overall sense of Anti-Semitism in the West, it is not any surprise that an even stronger fear of otherness was brewing, causing both unity and division, and these fears were plastered all over horror movies in the golden age of cinema.

Post-World War I, the immigration of Eastern Europeans into the United States was once again increasing and those already settled in the States who had already adopted the melting pot of American culture grew concerned that the pot would be tainted by a dash of the old country. Taking this mass hysteria a step further, author of *Projected Fears: Horror Films and American Culture* Kendall R. Phillips describes a new field of science developed in the early twentieth century, "eugenics, a pseudo-science that supposedly 'proved' that certain races were endowed with a hereditary superiority or inferiority." This "us versus them" anxiety is especially reflected in some of the first monster movies released by Universal Studios, the film adaptation of *Frankenstein* and its predecessor *Dracula* (1931).

What makes *Dracula* a better display of America's suspicion of Easter European immigrants compared to *Frankenstein* is that, like these immigrants, the Count looks like everyone else and, in fact, was a human being at one time; Frankenstein's monster was not born of a woman. Phillips explains that "Dracula's monstrousness is not immediately visible, the threat not immediately apparent. This fear of the unknown must have resonated deeply with an America that had grown increasingly fearful of others. [Dracula is able to stroll] through the streets of London unrecognized."

---

3. D'Olimpio, L. *Connecting With Frankenstein: Modern Monsters and Belonging.* Retrieved from https://www.theconversation.com

Certainly the villagers in the beginning of the story, resembling superstitious Americans in the 1930s, attempt to warn Renfield with hearsay. However, the rumors spread by the villagers are only confirmed when Renfield is hypnotized into madness followed by the luring of Mina, solidifying the wary beliefs of American patriots. Dracula's influence over others is reflective of the universal fear during this time of immigrants spreading their customs and political values throughout the nation, draining America of its Americanness.

There are many reasons why immigrants hold onto parts of their past and the culture from their country of origin. However, none are malicious. Sometimes it is for the sake of maintaining an individual identity or for the security of familiarity to survive in the midst of uncertainty. Dracula drinks blood for survival. Like immigrants, he wishes to be immersed into "normal" society, even going as far as to conceal his true self from the public. But he will always be a vampire, just as the Eastern European immigrants could not change their heritage. If Dracula cannot change his nature, perhaps he is no more a threat than immigrants seeking freedom and acceptance.

One Monster, Mass Hysteria

Upon entering the Cold War in the 1950s, America shifted from having many enemies and making generalizations about all Eastern European countries to having just one enemy, one monster: Communist Russia. The American patriotism of the 1930s and 1940s continued to be the golden standard of conformity into the new decade, but was stronger than ever due to an instilled fear of an invasion. Many Americans began investing in emergency kits, stocking up on canned goods and nonperishables, and designing bomb shelters. There were suspicions that fellow colleagues and neighbors could be spies sending government secrets back to Mother Russia. Meanwhile, science fiction films of the time complemented this mass hysteria with warnings of an invasion by a mothership full of little green men.

In this slightly modified version of the "us versus them" war, there was an adamant refusal of communication, refusal to understand and learn from the purposed other. Representing both sides of the Cold War was the 1951 film *The Thing From Another World,* in which the researchers represent the mass hysteria of Americans and the monster represents the Russians, who had their own concerns about the standoff with America. It is made clear in the film that both sides allow violence to do all of the talking.

"Listen, I'm your friend, look I have no weapons," says Dr. Carrington to The Thing. "I'm your friend. You're wiser than I, you must understand what I'm trying to tell you." Following this attempt at making friends of an enemy, the creature aggressively pushes Dr. Carrington aside to wreak havoc. The lack of warmth and emotion displayed by The Thing resembles the stereotypical image of Soviets perceived by Americans. According to *Projected Fears* author Kendall R. Phillips, The Thing is a "metaphor for the American dream—a nation capable of facing the challenge of the unknown and facing its own diversity and division, not through strength and knowledge alone, but through an abiding affection that bonds it together." However, the "American dream" quickly dies in this film as the researchers each become monsters to one another, due to an increasing mistrust of each other, much like that of American citizens side-eying anyone who may not appear to love their country enough. Don't question the government. Wave your American flags proudly. And "keep watching the skies."

Monsters, Materialism, and Militancy

In the first sixty years of cinema, horror films portrayed monsters—reflections of America's fears—as ungodly creatures, aliens, and bloodsucking newcomers. Conformity was more about keeping people out rather than barricading them inside. In the early 1960s, conformity could be defined by the collective and materialistic ideals introduced each day on television screens that encouraged Americans to get a job, buy a house in the suburbs, start a family, and wait to die. It was Alfred Hitchcock who revealed America's superficial expectations of normalcy as a claustrophobic vision of Hell in *Psycho* (1960). Norman Bates urged us to wake up from the American dream and to fear the status quo, fear the boy next door. While to many, the monster that carried us into this new decade of horror was the knife-wielding Freudian head case Norman, perhaps the real monster is the thing that helped make him that way: his dead mother's conformist values.

When Norman is first introduced in the film, he is already a walking PSA, warning of the consequences that come with actually achieving the suburbanite American dream. Because the homes that were being built and bought in the early 1960s were so grandiose in size and so far from civilization, keeping up with domestic chores became an overwhelming task for many women to accomplish on their own. For what may be the first time in history, many men shared the apron with their wives, taking on the burden of yard work and gardening, spending more time at home, and blurring the line between gender roles and expectations. Norman, of course, is seen taking on the role and responsibility of both man and woman of the house to the point of entrapment.

"A hobby is supposed to pass the time, not fill it," Norman says regarding his taxidermy work. Perhaps the real American dream is the mere desire for the *Leave It To Beaver* lifestyle. But once we have achieved the big house, the shiny career, and maybe produce a tiny human or two, then what? If you follow the logic laid out in *Psycho*, the answer is that boredom and isolation may drive out what little sanity you have left. "Norman has achieved the kind of isolated, protected life recommended by the suburban vision. His work is empty and meaningless, his life is confined to his private property, and he spends his time pursuing leisure" (Phillips, *Projected Fears*). Like Norman, many victims of conformity in the 1960s dreamed of an escape from their secluded domestic lives, but to admit discontent while encased in a white picket fence would be madness.

In the latter half of the decade, conformity and social norms shifted from an emphasis on superficiality, to a strengthened respect for authority and militancy. "When we look to the 1930s, 40s, and 50s, they shared a deep anxiety about things that might threaten the social order. Starting in the late 1960s, the focus shifted more to a sense that the social system was already failing," writes Phillips. As the Vietnam War began and barely-legal young men were swept from their suburban lives and dropped deep into the jungle, the youth of America found absurdity in those who followed orders and failed to ask questions, namely their zombie parents. Although the word "zombie" is never uttered in the 1968 film *Night of the Living Dead*, George A. Romero ensured that everyone watching knew what it meant to be one.

The undead wandering through the country and chewing on the brains of their fellow man and woman are symbolic of the mindless drones that Americans were expected to become if it were not for discussion and protest of the war. In the film, the living were the only hope for salvation. If only they could reprogram their minds to decide for themselves what is right, rather than turning to the authorities as if they have all the answers. "They'll tell us what to do," Ben says as he turns his attention to the news announcement on the television set. However, once the group of shut-ins begin following the advice of the man in the moving picture box, they risk being consumed by their new flesh-eating foes. Furthermore, the sole survivor in the farmhouse, Ben, who first suggested listening to authorities for survival, is gunned down by a gang of rednecks who are also doing as they have been told by authority figures. Romero's film demonstrates that the monsters are neither the walking dead nor the living, but those in power guiding the hands of the living until they become the walking dead.

Monsters and Family Values

Expanding on the anti-authority rebellion of the late 1960s, the 1970s heavily focused on specific authority figures: parents. During this decade, parental figures were often either absent from horror films, leaving their adolescent children to fight for their lives alone; or they were present and a part of the plot. Conformity was narrowed from obeying authority in general to obeying some very specific conservative rules: no sex, no drugs, no crazy teenage shenanigans. The monster in many films of the groovy 1970s stood in place of parents as an exaggeration of the perspective teens had on their parents. Only the good and pure survive. Many young ones might have uttered the phrase "My parents are going to kill me for doing that." In horror, parents don't punish, but someone—or something—will. Enter the slasher film.

In folklore, there have been dozens of tales about the "bogeyman" that have served as a warning to misbehaving children who must conform to the status quo or face the torturous consequences. Horror films such as John Carpenter's *Halloween* (1978) embraced such urban legends, transforming the monster from the outcasts created by conformists to enforcers of conformity themselves. There is an obvious absence of parents in this film in particular. Even young Michael Myers spends Halloween night without his parents and, left to his own devices (or vices?), he picks up a knife and commits his first murder. Without parents and without social order, Lynda and Bob got their hands on alcohol and each other. Annie didn't even have the chance to do anything of a forbidden nature before being asphyxiated as her intentions had already soiled her soul. And then there is Laurie Strode, the virgin, the kid-friendly girl next door, the girl scout. Sure, she accepts a joint from her pal Annie, but it's clear that she does not take pleasure from the activity, for she lacks a single deviant thought or intention. She's the daughter of every parent's dreams and she conquers all… even the bogeyman.

Tobe Hooper's *The Texas Chain Saw Massacre* (1974) perfectly exemplifies a vision of the lacking family values in the 1970s. The cannibalistic family of rednecks—a family still intact—displays chaos and insanity, immorality, and savage behavior as they come together to terrorize a group of parent-less teen hippies. *The Exorcist* (1973) also shines a light on the decline of the nuclear family that was held in such high regard during previous decades. Regan is raised by a single-working mother, absent a father. Like Michael Myers, she spends much of her time in solitude with a pathway to evil right at her fingertips. Without order and without authority figures to enforce it, conformity is restored through fear.

LIKE, TOTALLY INSECURE MONSTERS

When I was in my first semester of college, I took a course on the horror genre. As I received my class syllabus, I discovered something missing. There were not any sections on 1980s horror. Being the passionate fan that I am, I confronted my professor about this major gap in my education to which he responded with "The 1980s are kind of redundant. It's mostly repeats of the 1970s. Sequels."

Although the studios in the 1980s did in fact mass produce sequel upon sequel of the slasher films repeating the teen rebellion of the 1970s, a new kind of monster movie shared the spotlight in this decade. The totally bodacious '80s were overflowing with materialism, classism, and vanity. Americans aimed for big hair, big careers, and big bank accounts, all to the beat of dramatic drum-crashing soundtracks. Through these desires came severe insecurities such as the fear of aging, fear of dipping below the white collar status, fear of being different or abnormal according to the strict standards of fashion, beauty, and wealth. Monsters were not necessarily external but rather a reflection of our inner demons, and our inner demons tend to berate us for not being the very image of perfection. Our inner demons tend to push conformity for the sake of belonging and status.

According to journalist Kevin Harley in his article "What Makes Cinema's Greatest Monsters So Scary,"[4] "[David Cronenberg's *The Fly* (1986)] fused human and monstrous in an emotional meditation on aging." On the surface, Seth Brundle is merely a mad scientist transforming into a winged insect after an unfortunate experimental mishap. However, as we

---
4. http://www.gamesradar.com

watch this gradual mutation—the loss of fingernails, puss oozing from his once-smooth skin, the decay of everything that ever made Jeff Goldblum a heartthrob—we are joined together in this reminder that flawlessness is impossible and beauty is temporary.

Beauty standards were only the beginning of fear in the 1980s as Brian Yuzna's 1989 film *Society* acknowledged vanity's grotesque cousin, classism. All-American teenage boy Bill Whitney finds out that his family, as well as his neighbors and peers, are members of an orgy cult of deformed monsters made up of Beverly Hills socialites—and he is not one of them. Underneath the butt humor and scenes that cannot be unseen, *Society* contains a thick layer of intelligence in its portrayal of upper-class America and the greed that continues to divide socioeconomic classes. "Didn't you know, Billy boy, the rich have always sucked off low-class scum like you," says one of Bill's classmates before his tongue unravels from his mouth. Told from the somewhat cathartic point of view of the American working class, the film doesn't hold back when painting a portrait of those born into wealth and entitlement as being quite literally disgusting and inhuman.

Monsters and the Media

After the emergence of MTV and music video-soaked pop culture, the 1990s brought forth reality as entertainment. On May 21, 1992, the first episode of *The Real World* was plastered across every teen's television screen as they watched young adults just like them engage in sex, drugs, and debauchery. Seven years later, Columbine became a household name when two high school seniors, Eric Harris and Dylan Klebold, massacred twelve of their peers and one teacher before taking their own lives. Since then, there have been hundreds of similar incidents at schools all over the U.S. What all of these individuals have in common is that they were all showered with fame by the mass media, given a platform for committing heinous acts. To many, these are the names of monsters. But are the reporters, the news anchors, and the people behind the cameras not feedings these beasts? In the 1990s, it appeared the socially acceptable way of life was to seek your fifteen minutes of fame by any means necessary.

This love of voyeurism and spectacle was lightly observed in the 1991 film *Silence of the Lambs*. In his book *The Monster Show: A Cultural History of Horror*, David J. Skal writes:

Like Dracula, Hannibal Lecter has a pronounced taste for human blood; like Frankenstein, he is a brilliant but mad scientist; he has two personalities like Dr. Jekyll and Mr. Hyde, both civilized and savage; and like some side-show super-geek, he is held and exhibited in a succession of zoo-like enclosures.

Dr. Lecter is watched by guards, law enforcement, and the media like a bug under a magnifying glass, with only Clarice interacting with him as she would any human being. She never once relishes in his gory claims to fame, never once grants him that satisfaction. Meanwhile, Buffalo Bill is on the loose, casting a shadow on the cannibal's murderous accomplishments.

By the time Wes Craven's *Scream* landed in theaters in 1996, the youth of America was already on its way to desensitization from brutality. Billy and Stu are rather prophetic of the danger that many high schools would soon face. Insensitive and murder-obsessed, with absent parents, these two not only get their kicks from committing crimes just like in the movies, but also from giving the news anchors in their quiet community a reason to start shouting. However, the murders are perhaps just as thrilling for news reporter Gale Weathers, because they allow her a brief brush with fame. "The killers seek out the media attention, staging their murders in spectacular, almost artistic ways so as to draw attention, and in turn, the news reporters seem to hope for more carnage" (Phillips, *Projected Fears*). Journalists have a saying that "if it bleeds, it leads." Which monster is more bloodthirsty? The killer or the person holding the microphone?

WHO'S THE MONSTER NOW?

Shortly after ringing in the new millennium, just when the Y2K scare ended and we thought the world was safe, America returned to its fear of "the other" but on more general terms. On September 11, 2001, New York City was under attack as the Twin Towers were taken down by crashing planes. At the time, I was only twelve years old and lived on the other side of the country. I had never been to New York City, I had never heard of the Twin Towers, and I didn't know what Al Qaeda was but I was told that it was a group of bad people. When I was in seventh grade, there was a young Muslim girl in my classes who was born in America, spoke fluent English, and read all the same teen magazines as the rest of us. Every day, I witnessed my peers calling her "Osama Bin Laden." She was neither from the Middle East nor a member of Al Qaeda. From this moment, I knew that the millennium was now defined by division and that making generalizations about specific groups was the nation's way of conforming.

Our regression to separate-but-equal views has never been more apparent than in AMC's highly acclaimed television show *The Walking Dead*. According to University of Southern California Professor of English, Art History, and Film Leo Braudy, "While other monsters are individuals, there's no hierarchy in the zombie world, no 'king zombie,' so fear of zombies represents a modern fear of groups. They might be Islamic fundamentalists, immigrants, Republicans, Democrats—you name it, whatever group frightens you."[5] All zombies are a threat no matter the fact that they were once someone's mother or father, someone's significant other, someone's child. Especially in later episodes of the series, the group led by the crazed Negan can often be heard chanting "We are Negan," as if to say that Negan represents all of them. There are no physically unique qualities about them, no differing opinions or beliefs. We are supposed to assume that the entire group is inherently monstrous because of one bad apple.

Since the popularity of this series, several films have been released in the last twenty years that have driven home the idea of division and fear of groups. *Starry Eyes* withdrew the curtain from Hollywood studios, revealing those abusing power within the entertainment industry as a sinister cult before the #MeToo movement some years later. *Ex Machina* (2014) confronted our fear of a superior race rising to the surface and possibly leading to the ultimate demise of the humanity. Jordan Peele's *Get Out* (2017) opened our eyes to the continuing ignorance of Anglo-America.

Who are the real monsters in society? They are people. Those who follow the herd unaware of the destination. Those who cast out the "meek, the disenfranchised, and the marginalized."[6] And that is the most frightening reality.

---

5. Bell, S. "Monsters On Our Minds: What Our Fascination With Frightful Creatures Says About Us." Retrieved from https://www.news.usc.edu

6. David Harbour, 2017 SAG Awards

Biographies

Editors

Rebekah McKendry is an award-winning director, writer, and producer with a strong focus in the horror and science fiction genres. She has a doctorate in Media Studies focused on the Horror Genre from Virginia Commonwealth University, an MA in Film Studies from City University of New York, and a second MA from Virginia Tech in Arts Education. Rebekah previously worked as the Editor-in-Chief at Blumhouse Productions and as the Director of Marketing for Fangoria Entertainment. She was also a co-host of Blumhouse's award-winning Shock Waves Podcast and currently hosts the Colors of the Dark Podcast on the Fangoria Podcast Network.

Los Angeles native **Alyse Wax** is the daughter of a writer. So naturally, she rebelled and wanted nothing to do with the craft. Eventually, however, she grew up and realized that following in her mother's footsteps is not the worst thing in the world. A chance meeting led to a job at FEARnet, a top horror website and cable network. Alyse worked there for nearly seven years as a reporter and television critic, eventually becoming Associate Editor, before Kabletown shut down the popular site. Continuing with her passion for the horror and sci-fi genre, she is a regular contributor to SYFY WIRE, Collider, Coming Soon, and Bloody Disgusting. She was briefly the editor-in-chief of DreadCentral.com, and has written for Fangoria Magazine, Crave, IndieWire, and Daily Dead. Her work has also appeared in Teen People Magazine and Weekly World News.

Alyse is the author of two books: *Curious Goods: Behind the Scenes of Friday the 13th: The Series*, about the 1980s cult TV show; and *The World of IT*, an official behind-the-scenes look at the *IT* movies directed by Andy Muschietti.

A USC Film School graduate and former figure skater, you can follow Alyse on Twitter: @alysewax.

Cover Artist

Karen McKenna is an artist and independent game developer from New Jersey. She obsessively collects toys, spends too much time thinking about *The X-Files*, and has an affinity for cats. Follow her on Twitter: @RainKnight_Art.

Contributors

Rhianne Paz Bergado is a filmmaker and DJ based in Long Beach, California. As a second generation Filipino-American, Rhianne explores themes of intersectionality and culture told from her own unique perspective. You can find her film and television work at rhiannepaz.com and follow her DJ adventures on Instagram @donotfeedthedj.

Meredith Borders is the Managing Editor and Associate Publisher of the newly revived Fangoria magazine, where she achieved a lifelong dream by writing the cover story of Fango Vol. 2 Issue 1. She came to Fangoria as the former Editorial Director for Alamo Drafthouse, Fantastic Fest and Birth.Movies.Death. website and magazine, as well as a freelance writer and editor of nearly twenty years. Meredith and her husband Matt Schlabach own City Acre Brewing Company in Houston, Texas, where Meredith programs a monthly film series. You can find her byline at SlashFilm, Playboy, Bloody Disgusting and more, or follow her on Twitter at @xymarla. She was defending *Jennifer's Body* before it was cool.

Heather Buckley was a graphic designer and creative lead for thirteen years in New York advertising before transitioning to her life-long dream of working in the film industry. She worked in the makeup department on Billy Pon's *Circus of the Dead*, and then as Makeup FX Shop Supervisor on The Booth Brothers' SYFY channel film *Dead Still* (and, under prosthetics, played a featured ghoul) and Ted Geoghegan's *We Are Still Here*. She is an award-winning Blu-Ray Special Features Producer working on documentary projects for Red Shirt Pictures, Severin Films, Kino Lorber, Arrow Films and Lionsgate (over one hundred and counting), and was one of the producers on Jenn Wexler's *The Ranger* for Glass Eye Pix and Hood River Entertainment. Heather has also been a journalist for over a decade, contributing to Dread Central, Vulture and Fangoria. Follow her on Twitter and Instagram: @_heatherbuckley.

Kaydee Cage is a musician, teacher, and horror movie fanatic. Along with her four brothers, she was equally terrified and mesmerized by horror films such as *The Shining*, *The Fog*, and *Dark Night of the Scarecrow*. A defining horror moment came to her at the end of the original *The Fly*, when the human-headed fly, caught in the spider's web screamed "Help me! Help Me!" as it was about to be devoured by the spider. Then both were smashed with a rock. To a young Kaydee, this scene defined horror perfectly, and haunted her for many nights after.

As an adult, she came out to the world as transgender and began transitioning to female in 2016. By 2017 she was living full time as a woman. She continues to obsess over horror films both old and new, competing (and often winning) the Dead Right Horror Trivia contest held annually at Phoenix Fan Fusion. In recent years her taste in horror has shifted more heavily to the paranormal and she's become quite outspoken in her love of all things found footage.

BJ Colangelo is a trauma-informed educator, film analyst, and actress turned filmmaker. Known for her provocative real-life storytelling and hot-take analyses on gender and LGBTQ+ representation in horror films, BJ's work has been featured in numerous trades including Shudder, Fangoria Magazine, Bloody Disgusting, Vulture, Blumhouse, Medium, Birth. Movies.Death. and Playboy, just to name a few. She also co-hosts the podcast This Ends at Prom with her wife Harmony—analyzing cinema marketed toward teen girls. Find her on Twitter @BJColangelo.

Zena Dixon combines her love of fashion and her birthright to horror as a writer and social media expert. She has contributed to Dread Central, Wicked Horror, Bloody Disgusting, Florida Geek Scene and Real Queen of Horror. This love also spans behind the camera, where Zena has completed multiple short films and is gearing up for her feature film. Follow Zena on Twitter: @LovelyZena.

Paula Haifley is a producer, writer, and vintage enthusiast who has worked in film and television for over a decade. She's been in love with and terrified by horror since being subjected to three *Nightmare on Elm Street* films at a second grade slumber party. Paula still holds her film school's accolades both for first disemboweling in a student film and as intramural Chubby Bunny champ (at sixteen marshmallows). She loves monsters, rock and roll, and those forgotten late night movies that keep you awake. You can find Paula on Twitter @paulahaifley; Instagram @gangrenejean; on her website www.heyflea.com; at LA revival theaters arguing that Freddy is better than Jason; and at any dive bar with a good jukebox loudly insisting that *Time Cop* is the greatest film ever made.

Heather Hendershot is a professor of film and media at the Massachusetts Institute of Technology. Her most recent book is *Open to Debate: How William F. Buckley Put Liberal America on the Firing Line*. She is currently writing a book on network television coverage of the Chicago Democratic National Convention of 1968. She tweets at @ProfHendershot.

Heidi Honeycutt is a film programmer, film journalist, and film historian. She has a boring bio.

Sandy King is a writer, producer and CEO of Storm King Productions. She has produced films ranging from public service announcements on hunger awareness to a documentary on astronaut/teacher Christa McAuliffe for CNN, to major theatrical hits like *They Live* and *John Carpenter's Vampires*. More recently, she directed and produced the *John Carpenter Live Tour* film and produced the horror/thriller, *Crones*, for Blumhouse/Amazon, scheduled for release in early 2021.

Sandy is also the first woman founder of a comic publishing house. Through Storm King Comics, she has created and written the award-winning *Asylum* series, the multiple award-winning *Tales for a Halloween Night* anthologies, as well as *John Carpenter's Tales of Science Fiction*, and the graphic novel line *Night Terrors*. In December 2019, Sandy launched the new comics line, Storm Kids, offering comics for ages four to eighteen years old.

She is married to director John Carpenter and lives in Hollywood, California.

Carly Lane-Perry is the contributing editor for SYFY Wire FanGrrls, as well as a lifelong Star Wars fan, diehard romance reader, nascent horror lover, and dedicated live-tweeter. Her work can also be found at Nerdist, Teen Vogue, Bitch Media, The Mary Sue, Den of Geek, Motherboard, The Toast and elsewhere around the Internet. Follow her on Twitter @carlylane.

Sonia Lupher is a PhD candidate in Film and Media Studies at the University of Pittsburgh, where she is writing a dissertation on the ties between contemporary women's horror cinema and the history of women's cinema. She is the founder/project manager of *Cut-Throat Women: A Database of Women Who Make Horror* (cutthroatwomen.org), a project that aims to shed light on the role of women in horror film production. Her work has been published in *Critical Quarterly*, and she has also contributed to Bitch Flicks, Graveyard Shift Sisters, and Grim Magazine.

Los Angeles native **Erin Maxwell** grew up on the mean streets of West Hollywood. After a short stint in the Land of Entrapment for college, Erin has earned her keep as both a corporate shill and a scribe for trade mags and local rags. She is a pop culture guru with an encyclopedic knowledge of television, movies, comics, and animation thanks to her parents' reliance on cable television, an ancient Betamax, and a Nintendo gaming system as robot babysitters. And she loves the Haunted Mansion. Follow her on Twitter: @erinemaxwell.

Stacie Ponder is a New England swamp hag who writes and has written for Rue Morgue magazine, Arrow Video, Kotaku, and more, including her long-running horror blog Final Girl. She also co-hosts the queer feminist horror podcast Gaylords of Darkness.

Jamie Righetti is an author, screenwriter, and director from New York City. Her work has been featured on IndieWire, SlashFilm, One Perfect Shot, and her debut novel, *Beechwood Park*, is now available on Amazon. She loves horror, Martin Scorsese, *BioShock,* and her dog, Nugget. You can follow her on Twitter @JamieRighetti.

Debbie Rochon began her writing career penning a column for Joe Bob Briggs' bi-weekly publication The Joe Bob Report in 1996. Since then she has written for a myriad of horror and grindhouse themed magazines, including Fangoria, where she won the esteemed Rondo Hatton Classic

Horror Award for her column "Diary of the Deb" in 2014. Debbie has signed on with a publishing house to release her autobiography *From the Underbelly to the Underground* slated for a 2021 release.

Amy Searles regrets that she will not live long enough to watch all of the horror movies.

Chelsea Stardust has been a horror film fan since the age of ten when her father showed her George Romero's *Night of the Living Dead* and Tod Browning's *Dracula*. When she wasn't racing sled dogs in the snowy Midwest, Chelsea consumed all the cinema she could get her hands on. She attended Ohio University's Honors Tutorial College School of Film program where she focused on Directing, then found her horror home at Blumhouse Productions, where she served as the executive assistant to Jason Blum for several years. Since leaving her post at Blumhouse Productions, Chelsea has been directing full time. Her first short film, "Where Are You?" was part of the 2016 Etheria World Tour and was also featured on Nerdist's Short Ends on Alpha. She released four short films on Crypt TV, two of which have exceeded one million views, and directed the holiday-horror radio play "Christmas Eve" for Earbud Theater.

Chelsea also directed a horror/musical/comedy for the stage titled *Slashed! The Musical* for the 2017 Hollywood Fringe Festival, which was nominated for Best Musical, Screamiest Show and won the Encore Award. Chelsea's first feature film, the science fiction thriller *All That We Destroy*, is part of the Blumhouse series *Into The Dark* and is currently available on Hulu. Her second feature film is the horror comedy *Satanic Panic*, written by novelist Grady Hendrix, and produced by Fangoria and Cinestate. She is repped by United Talent Agency and Heroes & Villains Entertainment. Follow her on Twitter: @StardustChelsea.

Sarah Stubbs is an online content creator with a passion for all things pop culture, especially food and horror. Her mother taught her how to cook at a young age and was instrumental in her love of horror movies, showing her movies like *House on Haunted Hill* and all of the Universal Monster movies before the age of ten.

Sarah co-founded the site Geeks Who Eat (2geekswhoeat.com) with her husband Matthew in 2015. Having received a Bachelor of Arts in History (almost a requirement in her family of history majors), Sarah uses her research skills to find themes and elements that enhance the recipes created for and featured on Geeks Who Eat. The constant use of this type of research has given her a level of expertise in the intersection of food and pop culture. Long story short, movie night with Sarah is always extra. You can find her on Instagram and Twitter: @SpookySarahSays or @GeeksWhoEat.

Jenn Wexler is the director of *The Ranger*, which world premiered at the 2018 SXSW Film Festival and is now streaming on Shudder. She is the producer of Larry Fessenden's *Depraved* (WTF 2019), Ana Asensio's *Most Beautiful Island* (SXSW Grand Jury Prize 2017, Independent Spirit John Cassavetes Award Nominee 2018), Robert Mockler's *Like Me* (SXSW 2017), and Mickey Keating's *Psychopaths* (Tribeca Film Festival 2017) and *Darling* (Fantastic Fest 2015). Find her on Twitter @J_Wex and Instagram @BubblegumAndBlood.

www.ingramcontent.com/pod-product-compliance
Lightning Source LLC
Chambersburg PA
CBHW051926160426
43198CB00012B/2051